ME,

A ONE-ROOM COUNTRY SCHOOL TEACHER

Alberta, Canada, 1939 – 1945 and beyond

Memoirs of
A One-Room Country School Teacher

Alberta, Canada, 1939 – 1945 and beyond

By
Frances A. Clark Ruttan

Copyright © 2013 by Frances A. Clark Ruttan

All rights reserved. No part of this book may be reproduced, stored in a mechanical retrieval system, or transmitted in any form by any means, electronic, mechanical, video, laser, photocopying, recording means or otherwise, in part or in whole, without the written permission of the author.

ISBN-13: 978-1491000021
ISBN-10: 1491000023

Book design & production: Molly Ruttan-Moffat
Printed in the USA

I dedicate this book to my grandchildren

Devon, Sydney, Kelci, Lukas and Nina,

whose questions, interest and schooling

inspired me to write down my stories.

Table of Contents

Acknowledgments ix
Introduction xi

PART ONE
Alberta, Canada, 1939 – 1945

CHAPTER ONE
Practice Teaching 1

CHAPTER TWO
Atim Lake School 9

CHAPTER THREE
Earnest Park School 27

CHAPTER FOUR
Lone Ridge School 35

CHAPTER FIVE
Elk Point School 51

CHAPTER SIX
John Russell Elementary
School 57

PART TWO
THE STORY CONTINUES...
*Ontario, Canada and New
York, United States, 1946 – 1950*

CHAPTER SEVEN
The Ontario Religious
Education Council 75

CHAPTER EIGHT
Union Theological
Seminary 97

About the Author 109

ACKNOWLEDGMENTS

I would like to thank my children Bill Ruttan, Molly Ruttan-Moffat, Linda Ruttan-Moldawsky, their families, my dear friend Bernice Delugach and fellow-writer Kerry Madden, all of whom read many of my early drafts, and have given me endless support and encouragement.

I would also like to thank my sister Nancy Harsh for the use of her letter from her stay at Lone Ridge School, and for providing some of the pictures.

Finally, a special thanks to Kathy Tomlinson, for joyfully editing the "Part One" manuscripts, to Molly, for putting my stories and pictures together to create this book, and to Linda, for writing the back-cover blurb.

Introduction

Before the 1950's there were few city schools in Alberta, Canada. Since the majority of children lived on farms scattered across the province, it was decided by the "powers that be" that no child should have to walk more than three miles to school. Consequently countless one-roomed country schools (grades one through nine) sprang up to meet the educational needs of these children. Today these students would be bused to a Consolidated School, or taught at home with the help of home-schooling material provided by the province.

Many of the teachers had themselves attended one-room country schools, and felt at home in them. For the few of us who had attended a city school with it's separate grade levels (including me), the environment of having one classroom for children of all grade levels was a new experience and a real challenge.

Part One of this book is an account of my teaching (and learning) experience in three one-room country schools, as well as two accounts of my teaching in small Alberta schools.

In 1946 I began my employment with the O.R.E.C. (Ontario Religious Education Council) as a Children's Work Secretary, which involved travel throughout Ontario to help churches associated with the organization with their children's religious educational programs. Part Two continues with my experiences working with the O.R.E.C., and concludes with the year I spent attending Union Theological Seminary at Columbia University in New York City.

Part One

Alberta, 1939 – 1945

CHAPTER ONE

"PRACTICE TEACHING"

District of Cloverdale, Alberta
1939

In the year nineteen hundred and thirty nine I decided to become a teacher. Fresh from a city high school and before that a city grade-school, in September of that year I enrolled in a teacher training program at the Alberta Normal School in Edmonton, Alberta. To complete this program, my classmates and I needed to learn to become a teacher, principal, and manager of a one-room country school, all in the span of nine short months. Toward that end, our mentors mandated that not only should we be schooled in the latest and best that the fields of psychology and pedagogy had to offer, but also that we should spend two one-week periods in one-roomed country schools to discover how things were really done! The following September we would all find ourselves in one of these schools. For most Normal School students, who had attended rural schools, this would be a familiar environment, but those of us like me, who had not, it would be a different world.

In those days there were few city schools in Alberta, or in all of Canada for that matter. Schools having one classroom for each grade, or even one classroom for as few as three grades, were found only in cities or small towns. One-roomed schools, serving children in grades one through nine, were built to serve rural farming communities. They were usually no farther than six miles apart to ensure that no child would have to walk farther than three miles to school. Because high schools were found only in the towns, it was common for high-school students from farms located far away to seek board with a friend. Others walked a long way each day or rode horseback to attend a high school. Even more left school altogether after completing the ninth grade. The boys, especially, were needed to work in the fields.

As part of my Normal School training, I was scheduled to "practice teach" in a rural one-room country school. Armed with the addresses of the school and the farmhouse where I was to stay, my father drove me out of Edmonton and into the country. About an hour's time down the highway and past the town of Cloverdale, we found the house. It was a large, classic farmhouse, set back from the road, with several well-kept small buildings around it. I knocked and was greeted, then shown to a neatly but sparsely furnished room, which had probably housed student teachers since the whole system began. The next morning I made my way to the school.

Super neat, the school was run by a young efficient teacher, who handed out previously prepared assignments to me with an air of having done this many times before. I remember trying to carry out these instructions under her watchful eye, and with the cooperation of her well-disciplined children. To the great amusement of this teacher, I had brought from Edmonton ten aspirin tablets — two for each day. I don't remember if I took them, but I probably did. What

I *do* recall is that my critique arrived a week or so after my stint there. It reported that she had been less than impressed by my performance. That was discouraging to me, but the Normal School staff seemed to think it par for the course. Looking back now I suspect that few good reports of student teachers ever came from that teacher.

My next practice teaching assignment was a very different story. Once again my father and I started out in the family car, early on a Sunday evening in April, to find where I was to be billeted. This time it took many inquiries along the way before we found a small, somewhat shabby house, situated along a back road and down a long driveway. It was almost ten o'clock and quite dark, when we arrived.

There were no visible lights. We opened the only gate we could find, and picked our way to the only door there seemed to be. I stumbled up some steps leading to a low porch, and fell over something large and soft. Whatever it was rose, slowly, then moved over a few inches. In the gloom we felt, rather than recognized, a huge dog. Our exclamations of surprise and dismay alerted the farmer and his wife that the visiting teacher had finally arrived. (Their St. Bernard promptly went back to sleep!) A light materialized from somewhere. My father stayed long enough to make sure we had found the right house then left me to my fate.

My hosts greeted me, then led me through a shed-like room full of milking equipment. Pails, sinks, hoses, and a large cream separator crowded the little space. A second door opened to reveal the living room, furnished with a big round table, an overstuffed couch and chairs, a standing lamp, and a radio. Off this main room were two bedrooms, one belonging to my host and hostess, and the other to the school teacher.

It seemed I was to room with the teacher, and, as I soon discovered, share her bed as well. Unfortunately, since it was after ten p.m., she had already gone to bed. Obviously my late arrival was keeping my hosts up (though not the teacher). I said good night as expeditiously as possible, before disappearing with my suitcase, which contained, among other necessities, ten aspirin tablets, two for each day. In the darkened room I groped through my bag for pajamas, then crawled into bed next to the teacher, who woke up just long enough to say a groggy "hi," before going back to sleep. We introduced ourselves in the morning! And that was the beginning of a wonderful week.

Louise Moore was an ordinary sort of person, not young, but certainly not old, neither thin nor fat, not pretty, but easy to look at, and she dressed with no style at all. Her philosophy of life matched her casual appearance. She had neither dreams nor plans for the future (at least none that she shared with me), nor nostalgia for the past. It was against her principles to hold onto mementos, including snapshots. That struck me as odd and rather sad. As far as I could tell, she had no friends, and she avoided talk about her family.

Looking back on those days, I wish I had been able to learn more about her and from her. But at that time, managing my own life consumed all my energy. I liked her just the way she was, probably because she accepted me just the way I was. Unlike the previous teacher with whom I had worked, she had no special expectations of me, nor did she worry about her role in judging my performance. She made me feel wonderfully free and competent. It was fun and

Chapter One / "Practice Teaching"

satisfying to work with her, as well as walk back and forth to her school and roam the pastures, after an early supper, taking care to avoid the "cow pies."

The school reflected the personality of its teacher. The children were relaxed in a classroom that was neither tightly efficient nor sloppy. When the children arrived, they found places for lunch boxes, depositing them in a haphazard manner. No big deal! The same went for coats and boots, as well as for the few games and the odd bits of sports equipment the school possessed.

Louise taught with little imagination. She worked through the basic prescribed curriculum, and the children worked through the basic prescribed materials. Assignments were casually written on the blackboard. As the day progressed, she moved from one grade to another, back and forth, dealing with this situation and that, as it came up. No big deal! She put me to work doing the same. She accepted the children as they were, without agonizing over their pasts, present, or futures, and I felt a peace in that school that was totally lacking in the one I had worked in before.

Three incidences from this school have stayed with me. One morning just as the children were arriving, a Royal Canadian Mounted Police officer appeared at the door. Louise paled, and seemed tense. The officer asked for her permission to talk to the children about safety rules they should follow when walking along the highway on their way to school. Louise relaxed, and I saw her eyes fill with tears. She told me later that she had been afraid he had come to tell us that one of our students had been hit by a car.

The second incident involved a new report card format issued by a progressive education department of the provincial government, for use in all rural schools. Louise had recently sent the new card to parents for the first time. It replaced their short, one-page card that listed Math, Reading, Language, Social Studies, and Spelling beside boxes for grading A, B, C, D, or F, as well as spaces for teacher comments and a parent's signature. Their new card was long and detailed. Among other things, it divided each subject into sub-categories, which was confusing enough. But worse still, instead of A, B, C, D, and F, which everyone understood, this card designated grades of "above average," "satisfactory," and "needs special help."

Children and parents alike were thrown into confusion. The report cards were being returned the week I was there, and the children were clamoring with questions. *What* special help, by *whom,* and *where?* Louise took the time to clear things up.

"Children," she said, "If you get scolded a lot because your work is not right, or you have to keep doing it over, that is what *special help* means!"

So much for the new report card! I was glad that the bright, young educator, who had dreamed up this new card for the board of education, was not there to hear Louise's explanation for "special help." On the other hand, maybe that is exactly where he should have been.

The third incident involved another form, one to be filled in by the children. It was an attractive chart sent out by the Junior Red Cross, listing all the days of the year with tiny spaces to be checked off if certain daily health habits had been performed, such as "brushed my teeth." Each day the children pulled their cards from their desks and checked off the appropriate spaces. When I walked between the

Chapter One / "Practice Teaching"

desks, watching this activity, I noticed that one little boy had filled in the squares for "slept with my window open" right through spring, summer, and fall.

Since it was now only Spring, I called him on this. How could he be sure he would sleep with his window open on all those nights yet to come? He answered that he had broken his window, and his father had declared he would not fix it until winter set in.

Well, so be it. I hoped the screen was still intact. Mosquitoes were brutal in rural Alberta, spring, summer, and fall.

Louise gave me a good report; not glowing, but good, because she liked me. Maybe she suspected that I might have trouble managing a school of my own, but she wasn't much interested in my future, and anyway, when all was said and done, I had to make my own mistakes and learn to swim on my own.

The next time I found myself in a one-roomed country school, I was on my own, totally. It was Atim Lake School, about twenty miles west of Edmonton, near Spruce Grove. I went full of confidence and dreams, but that teaching year turned out to be one of my hardest. In fact, that year in general was one of the most challenging of my life. It was the year that my failures, as well as my successes, helped shape me into the experienced teacher I would eventually become.

At University Ski Hill, Edmonton, circa 1939.

On my bike with Rainy the dog, circa 1939.

CHAPTER TWO

ATIM LAKE SCHOOL

Spruce Grove, Alberta
September 1939 – June 1940

The summer of nineteen hundred and thirty nine found me looking for my first teaching position. Canada was at war, which made for a teacher shortage. Many young men who might otherwise be teaching were involved with the war in one way or another. The Stony Plains Consolidated School Board encouraged me to sign on with them, and in no time I was appointed to a school named Atim Lake, about twenty miles west of Edmonton near the small town of Spruce Grove.

Once again my father and I drove out into the country to locate the school and to find a place for me to live. We saw a nice-looking farmhouse directly across the road from the school. The family there said they would be happy to board the new teacher, but that I would have to "bunk in" with one of their girls. Having experienced "bunking in" while practice teaching, I decided to pass up that offer. Later, I was told that this family had nineteen children, ten of whom still lived at home. It was no wonder the teacher could not expect to have a bed of her own in their home, let alone a room! The next house down the road could not take in the teacher either, but suggested that we try "The Hagens."

The Hagens' house turned out to be a little cottage on a small farm, both of which had seen better days. I was immediately drawn to Mrs. Hagen, a diminutive worn-out-looking woman who turned out to have been the first teacher of Atim Lake School, twenty-five years before. She had taught the first of the above-mentioned nineteen children. I discovered later that I was to have the last two, Ruth and Gordon.

The house was divided into six areas: a good-sized kitchen, dominated by a large, wood-burning cook stove; a space next to the kitchen for a cot, which functioned as a bedroom for the Hagens' son, Don; a lean-to at the other side of the kitchen that housed a pump and washroom, (there was no running water, plumbing, or electricity); the main room, a combined living/dining room; and two

The Hagen's daughter, Kathleen, standing in front of the Hagen's cottage.

very small bedrooms, one of which became mine. In my room, there was just enough space for a cot-sized bed, a straight-backed chair on which rested a small coal-oil lamp, a chest of drawers, and a row of hooks for hanging clothes. All the essentials!

My footlocker went under my bed for extra storage space, and under the window I put the only piece of furniture I brought from home — a book box that my father had made for me. Removing its lid transformed it into a small bookcase. Over the next ten years, that book box, decorated with shipping labels from across Canada and the United States, would go with me to every job I was to hold.

I have only warm memories of that year with the Hagens. Mrs. Hagen became my mentor and friend during the difficult months ahead. I grew very fond of her and her daughter, Kathleen, who livened up the weekends when she returned from her job in Edmonton. Don set off each morning on his horse Shorty, for the five-mile ride to his school. During the fall hunting season he shot prairie chickens from his saddle. I made the mistake of assuring his mother that I liked to eat prairie chicken, which resulted in prairie-chicken sandwiches in my lunch every day for well over a month.

Mr. Hagen, a man of few words, seemed to carry with him a permanent air of depression. He had little good to say about the world in general and farming in particular, but there was something endearing about him, maybe because he was so obviously fond of his wife and proud of his children. He would end each breakfast by rising up with a big sigh, and saying, "Well, I guess I had better go feed them pigs."

My days followed a predictable pattern. Every morning I woke to the sound of Mr. Hagen shaking down the coals from yesterday's fire

I set out for the mile-long walk to school.

in the Franklin stove (which was just outside my bedroom door) in preparation for the new day's fire. This stove and the kitchen range were the only sources of heat in the poorly insulated house.

As soon as water had been heated on the kitchen stove, (Mrs. Hagen's first chore of the day), she would bring some to me in a large china pitcher and place it on top of the dresser in an equally large china bowl. (Such bowl and pitcher sets, commonly used during the first part of the century, can now be found in antique stores all across the country.) Knowing the water would cool quickly was a great incentive for me to get up and get on with my morning toilet, which included a dash outside to the only outhouse available for the entire family. No store-bought toilet tissue. Torn pages from last year's Sears catalog did the trick.

For emergencies, I was provided with a "honey bucket" stowed under my bed, but I preferred the out-of-doors, and managed that cold dash all through the winter, even when the temperature dipped well below zero. Of course, my own personal plumbing was in great shape in those days, as were my eyes, for I remember reading *Gone with the Wind* (which had only recently been published) by the light

Chapter Two / Atim Lake School

of my coal-oil lamp, while stretched out on my stomach under the blankets, trying to keep warm.

After breakfast I would set out along a narrow country road for the mile-long walk to school. I remember so well that walk, which was lined with woods, fields of grain, barbed-wire fences, meadowlarks singing from fence posts, and two farmhouses. As the months went by, the woods first turned yellow, then a leafless brown. Fields became stubble, then covered with snow. The road became frozen and snow-packed, and it remained in that condition all winter long, until a late spring would finally arrive. Few birds were seen or heard. They had all flown south for the winter. The people who emerged from houses would appear in heavier and heavier clothing as the days became shorter and colder.

I wish I could say that this walk to school fed my soul (and maybe in some way it did), but all I remember is worrying about how I could handle my teaching job for the day ahead. On the way back,

The country road in the winter.

I pondered over what I could or should do differently the next day. At least I had an uninterrupted half-hour with my own thoughts, because Bessie, the only one of my pupils who took the same route, refused to walk with me. She kept a quarter mile ahead or behind, which both hurt and amused me, since I knew the reason behind this behavior. She did not want the older girls at school, who were carrying on a power struggle with me, to see her fraternizing with the teacher. On weekends, when she came to the Hagens' house to visit with Kathleen, there was nothing but goodwill all around.

A few of the children lived close to the school, but most of them had a long way to go — some almost three miles. Several traveled on horseback. One family came in a horse-drawn wagon, but the rest walked. Every country school had a horse barn. For those with horses, the first chore of the day was to shelter and care for their animals.

All the children carried their lunches in six-gallon lard pails, and all

Recess in the fall.

the lunches were alike. Each mother made sandwiches with thickly cut slices of bread filled with thickly cut meat, usually bologna. They were cut in quarters then tossed into the pail until it was full. No wrappings or zip-lock bags! There surely must have been a cookie or two, but I don't remember seeing many sweets or fruit. Not even raisins. I do remember the quantity and thickness of the sandwiches and watching with amazement as one little boy took his sandwich apart, then ate it layer by layer, because together it was too thick to get into his mouth. The children dipped into their lunch pails on their walk to school, opened them up for a snack at morning recess, and ate the bulk of the contents for lunch. They saved enough for a treat during the afternoon recess, and ate whatever was left on the way home.

All that September the weather was beautiful. The children ate outside, picnic style, on the grassy school ground, or just outside it, where there was a beautiful shady spot in the woods. But on the first day of October it turned cold, and before the month was over winter was upon us. As the days grew colder, my students' clothing became increasingly bulky.

But in November, December, January, and February, there were many days so cold that even the heaviest outfits failed to protect those who had a long way to walk. Hands and feet were the hardest to keep warm. The younger children would cry pitifully as their hands and feet began to thaw out and the pain intensified. But they were used to this, and there was little any of us, not so afflicted, could do, except hold small fingers and toes with our warm hands, and empathize until the pain subsided, tears dried up, and school could begin.

Recess in the winter.

As I look back on those days, I marvel that parents allowed those young children to walk such distances in those bitterly cold months with temperatures as low as 30 degrees below zero. They risked suffering severely from frostbite. I would never have allowed a child of mine to walk more than three blocks under those conditions. But these were first-generation Canadian children born to German immigrant parents, who valued above all, education, hard work, endurance, and authority. Only severe illness kept anyone from his appointed task, which for children was school.

Our school was always warm because one of the many young men who lived across the road came several hours before the opening of school to shake down, light, and stoke our coal-burning furnace. When the weather fell below zero, he would be over several times a day to keep it going. Of course, there was no heat during the night. Any liquid left in the classroom, such as paint and ink, would be frozen solid by morning.

Chapter Two / Atim Lake School

Back at the Hagens' house, Kathleen was still coming home on those wintry weekends, and when she was home, the family sleeping arrangements differed. The only extra bed was a Murphy bed that folded down from an outside wall in the space behind the kitchen, where Don usually slept on a cot. When Kathleen was home, Don would sleep with his father in the bedroom, while Kathleen and her mother shared the Murphy bed. It figures that the men landed the best deal! On several occasions that winter, I saw with horror that when the Murphy bed was lowered, its metal frame was thick with frost, which meant that the mattress must be icy cold through and through. The women would try to warm things up with hot-water bottles, but even when snuggling up tight together they shivered most of the night.

The Hagens had a very old car that they seldom used, except to drive into Spruce Grove for provisions. It had no heater or antifreeze,

A student from school, Mrs. Hagen and Kathleen Hagen play with a dog at the cottage.

Free time in the classroom.

an inconvenience that was easily overcome, I soon found out. One weekend, Don persuaded Kathleen and me to go to a high-school party. We piled into the car on a very cold winter night, wrapped in blankets for the long five-mile drive to Spruce Grove. The schoolyard was full of cars when we arrived, and the first thing Don did was drain the engine water into a container he had brought from home, then remove the car battery. We lugged the container and the battery into the school, where I discovered, to my astonishment, that the hall was lined with pails of water and car batteries as far as the eye could see. Well almost! It was a well-attended party.

It amazes me as I look back on that year that so little help was provided for beginning teachers, fresh out of Normal School. We found ourselves alone with as many as 40 children and the nearest house one-quarter mile away. Of course, most of the new teachers

Chapter Two / Atim Lake School

The children at their desks.

had been taught in similar schools throughout their childhood, and they knew from those experiences how it was done. As one of the instructors at Normal School was fond of saying, "Teachers teach as they were taught, and not as they were taught to teach." It's a good thing they did, because it was the only way they got through their first year of teaching. Oh, the school board did send an inspector twice a year, once in the fall and once in the spring, to make sure these new teachers were performing satisfactorily — and to help? Well maybe, but I was never made aware of that possibility. The word "inspector" was more likely to send chills down the spines of teachers and pupils alike, than to suggest the promise of help and encouragement.

Sometime in November, Mr. Hollinsworth, the inspector as well as the superintendent of the Stoney Plain School Board, made his fall visit to our school, taking me completely by surprise. I was working with one of the grades, when without warning all the children were out of their seats running around, and energetically straightening up things. Before I could ask, "What is going on?" one of them shouted, *"the inspector!"*

Someone had told me that when the inspector came to a school he inspected the outhouses first to give the teacher a few minutes to compose herself. The children were evidently aware of this, because they took these few precious minutes to tidy up the classroom. They dashed around, straightening up piles of papers and books. Coats, boots, and lunch pails went into neat rows, and any debris on the floor flew into the wastebasket. While I stood with my mouth hanging open in shock, someone said, "He's back," at which point they all fell into their seats with straight backs and folded hands. I suddenly realized that these children thought Mr. Hollinsworth had

Two girls play on a wooden xylophone that the teacher (I!) made.

come to inspect *them*, not *me*. They were doing this for *themselves*, rather than for me. It was the most satisfactory school day to date.

The inspection went well for me. My pupils were on their best behavior. They were super attentive, polite, and eager to show what wonderful kids they were. The inspector was impressed. He told me what a great class I had, how friendly, neat, and attractive the room looked, and how well behaved and cooperative the children were. I never let on that I was having problems. In due time, my inspector's report came. It was good, *very* good.

That same month, the children started to talk about "The Christmas Concert." Every year each of the rural schools put on a show, which everyone attended. And I mean *everyone*. It was the biggest entertainment and social function of the year. Part of the early planning was to find a date that no other school within reach had chosen, because everyone liked to go to all the other schools' productions (and compare notes)! I was not sure I had any special talent, but if I did, it certainly wasn't in the area of planning and directing a show. Besides, nothing was said about this in Normal School! Not to worry! The older girls put their heads together and came up with ideas, the main one of which was a "drill." I had never *heard* of this type of drill let alone *directed* one. Each drill turned out to be a combination of dancing and marching. The girls produced a book full of drills for me to look over with the one marked that they wanted to perform. I took the book home to study it.

Their first choice was called "The Rose Drill." It involved the girls wearing white cheesecloth dresses decorated with red crepe-paper roses while holding wands also adorned with such roses as well as

21

a rope so covered with the roses that it looked as if it was made of them. I was appalled. We couldn't possibly make all those roses, nor find the rope, nor make the dresses. I didn't even know how to make a rose out of crepe paper.

A meeting was called during our lunch break the next day. I vetoed the idea of the rose drill and suggested one I thought we could manage. The girls were incensed that I should be so unfeeling toward their wishes. At some sort of signal that I failed to detect, they got out of their seats and, without a word to me, retired to the playground. The meeting was over.

Well, not quite. A delegation came back with an ultimatum. Either I would agree to the rose drill, or they would not cooperate with any of my suggestions for our program. A strike, no less! It seemed to me that I had no option but to establish my authority. Like it or not, I was the teacher-principal of this school with total responsibility for what went on in it, and they were in my care. When they came back in to hear my verdict, I told them that unless they were able to accept and cooperate with whatever decisions I might make concerning the program, we could not have a Christmas Concert. They were to go home, think about it over the weekend, talk it over with their parents if they wanted to, and we would decide the next school day.

That was the worst weekend I had spent in my life (at least so far!) I agonized over my ultimatum. What was I thinking! What were the parents thinking? How could this new young teacher *cancel* a Christmas program that was a tradition? It was an important event in the life of the community. When I shared my dilemma with Mrs. Hagen, she was comforting, understanding, and supportive,

Chapter Two / Atim Lake School

Atim Lake School class picture.

and she did not seem unduly upset.

When Monday came, I hated to go back to school, but I had to. As soon as my ringleader girls arrived, they approached me and assured me that they *wanted* a Christmas program and that they would go along with *whatever* I decided. Looking back on this event, I strongly suspect that not word of our confrontation was shared with a parent, and the girls wanted to keep it that way. The girls knew better. German parents always sided with the going authority — especially with teachers.

I called another meeting during the noon break and shared with them my concerns about the rose drill. How could we come up with hundreds of roses? No problem! They had aunts and cousins and older sisters who knew how to make paper roses. In fact, they knew how to do it themselves.

What about the white cheesecloth dresses? No problem! Farm homes had cheesecloth on hand (for making cheese?), and if not, they knew where to get some. Mothers would make the dresses. Rope? It seemed there was plenty of rope hanging around a farm.

Sometime later, Mrs. Hagen told me that she'd heard from friends that during those weeks before Christmas there were red roses scattered around every room in every home in our school district! When the day of the Christmas program arrived, we had ropes, dresses, and wands, covered thickly with red roses — hundreds and hundreds of them in all shapes and sizes.

We had our Christmas program about a week before Christmas. Everyone came from miles around. All the desks (which were permanently attached to two-by-four skids) were pushed to one side or to the back of our classroom. Parents and guests sat on desk seats, desktops, or on the floor.

Besides performing the Rose Drill, the children sang some of the many songs I had taught them, for I loved to lead group singing. We did some simple skits, and my sister, bless her, who plays the violin beautifully, came to help with the music. It was a simple production, but the parents seemed happy, and the children were proud. Did we serve refreshments? Give out treats? Probably. But here my memory fails. That part of the evening must have gone smoothly!

One day in January, when the weather had stayed below zero for a long time, one of my first graders, Sophie, came to me visibly upset. Her story was that she could not sit down in the girls' outhouse because it was "too sharp." It hurt to use it, and she needed to "go." I had no idea what she was talking about and asked her to show me the problem. To my amazement and chagrin, since I should have been inspecting the outhouses on a regular basis as one of my duties, I was shown an inverted icicle, which poked up and beyond the hole where a child had to sit. We found a stick and knocked the thing down. An easy solution! The boys never seemed to have that problem. I suspect they could create new icicles whenever it became expedient — or just for fun.

When the time came for the inspector's spring visit, I was older, wiser, and weary. The ninth graders were facing provincial exams, which they had to pass in order to get into high school, and they were continuing to fight me by at least *pretending* they didn't care what I said or what I planned for them to study. I was worried for them and for me. The morning went well the day the inspector came, but after lunch I leveled with him about how hard it was for me to reach the teenagers and win their respect and confidence, which was crucial if I was to help them prepare for these important exams. He listened well and thoughtfully.

When the children came back after lunch he lit into these ninth graders about the importance of them qualifying for high school. He brought them up to the blackboard and tested them with hard questions, to demonstrate how much they had to learn in the short time that was left to them. Things were somewhat better after that, and as far as I know, all of my ninth-grade students passed the entrance exams and went on to high school, except for one boy, who dropped out to work in the fields with his father despite my best efforts to keep him in school. My second inspector's report was not as glowing as the first, but it was satisfactory, nonetheless.

Spring came, and the long stretch of road I walked on the way to school turned from snow to mud. The trees budded out in leaves, and farmers began to prepare their fields for seeding. Our birds returned — robins, meadowlarks, blue jays, woodpeckers, cedar waxwings. We made a list of them on the blackboard, as the children reported each new arrival.

There is little more I can, or care to, remember about that year at Atim Lake School. However, one day in particular, June 8, 1940, is engraved in my memory. I wrote D-Day in big letters on the blackboard and then told the children it was a day we would remember for the rest of our lives. It was the day the Allied forces crossed the English Channel and invaded France. All that year we had been well aware of the war going on. It had claimed many older brothers and friends. We sang the patriotic songs we heard on the radio, inserting "Canada" for "America" when possible, since Canada was completely out matched when it came to patriotic war songs.

The highlights for me that year were telling stories to the younger children, singing with the whole school, and reading books out loud, such as *Call of the Wild, Tom Sawyer,* and *Treasure Island.* I left at the end of the year relieved that I would be trading my role as teacher for one as a student at the University of Alberta, where I would soon begin to work towards a Bachelor of Arts degree. Still, I was convinced that the next time I found myself teaching in a one-room country school, I could, and would, do a better job. The person who had grown and learned the most that year, had been the teacher herself.

Chapter Three

Ernest Park School

District of Wetaskiwin, 1941

It was the spring of nineteen hundred and forty-one. My first university year, which had begun the fall of 1940, was over, and it was time to get back to teaching. In Alberta, as in most of Canada, college terms ended late in April, but grade schools kept going until the end of June. This meant that teachers attending the universities were available to substitute in schools (mostly rural schools) for the two months left of the school year.

Every year teachers were needed to take over for those teachers who for various reasons had hung on until relief was in sight. This opened up an opportunity for me to see if I could learn from past failures, prove to myself that I could teach a classroom of children, and — I hoped — even enjoy it.

Assuring myself that I could survive any classroom for only two months, I signed up to be the teacher for Ernest Park School, a one-room rural school near the town of Wetaskiwin, about 40 miles south, and west of Edmonton. The teacher who was vacating her post was reported to have had a "nervous breakdown." Not very reassuring news!

This time, since the school board had found me a place to live, I managed to get to my assigned post without the help of my father. I took two buses from Edmonton, the second of which deposited me (as well as my book box and footlocker) by the side of the road in the middle of nowhere. To my great relief someone was there to meet me — my new landlord, Ray, who drove me to an attractive two-story farmhouse on a small, but prosperous-looking, farm.

Ray and Ellen were a newly married couple having a "fun time" getting to know each other while learning to function as a working team creating a home, and running a farm. Both of them had been brought up on farms, but this particular farm seemed new to them. They embraced me as one of the family, and we quickly became friends.

"Sweetheart" Ray and Ellen.

Ellen called Ray "Sweetheart," which struck me as somewhat hilarious. Not that he wasn't a sweetheart — he was. It was just that due to my conservative upbringing, I had never heard a wife call her husband anything apart from his given name. Ellen would go out on the back porch, many times during the day, to call out instructions, such as "Sweetheart! Sweetheart!

It's time for lunch!" And, "Sweetheart" would appear.

The first time I saw "Sweetheart" prepare his favorite breakfast, my mouth dropped open in amazement. First, he filled a large bowl with freshly popped popcorn. Next he poured himself a cup of coffee, adding cream and sugar. Then, lifting his cup as if to drink, he poured the entire contents over the popcorn, and proceeded to eat it as if it were a bowl of cereal. Which indeed it was!

Ray and Ellen had an intriguing team approach when it came to milking the cows. Ellen did the actual milking, while Ray sat on the fence close by and read to her from the Bible. The first time I saw them do this, I vowed to myself that I would never let any future husband of *mine* get away with *that* sort of thing.

Well, about ten years later, I was married, and one day while I was vacuuming the rug, my husband started following me around reading jokes from the *Reader's Digest*. I said nothing, but my mind flew back to that barnyard scene. So much for pre-marital vows!

One day, Ray and Ellen announced that the time had come to butcher a pig and that someone, who was evidently an expert at this sort of thing, was coming to do the job. I decided to make myself scarce. It's one thing to like ham and bacon, but quite another thing to be party to the process by which it comes to the table. However, I wasn't to be let off that easily.

Later that day there was a festive gathering of family and friends to watch the big event: the cutting up of the pig into manageable pieces. I was soon to understand the term "cuts" as it refers to meat. Reluctantly and under considerable pressure, I joined the group, and I must confess that it was educational in a macabre sort of way. Having dissected earthworms and frogs in the zoology lab at the university, I could relate to this somewhat.

The pig was mounted on the barn wall, rather than pinned to a pad on a lab table. The head had been removed and all of the blood had been drained. Using a long, sharp scalpel, the so-called expert cut a huge Y-shaped incision down the belly of the pig and laid bare all the internal organs — heart, lungs, liver, intestines, etc. These were removed, one by one, for later disposition, after which the carcass was taken down from the wall, and the cutting into pieces began. The expert was paid in cuts of meat. I left as soon as I knew I could slip away unnoticed.

Ernest Park School comprised about twenty-five children, representing all grades except the ninth. Most of them seemed to be eight- to ten-year-old boys. Perhaps it only seems that way because

Students arriving on horseback.

Chapter Three / Ernest Park School

A game of softball in the schoolyard.

these boys were the only children there who gave me any grief. They were very rowdy on the school ground and got into a great many fights. I was constantly having to sort this out and finally realized that one boy in particular, Jim, seemed to instigate the confrontations. More often than not this led to someone being really hurt. Loss of recesses and numerous time-outs didn't help Jim change his ways, so finally, I applied *the strap*.

Corporal punishment was legal in those days. In fact, the strap — a piece of thick leather, about two and a half inches wide and a foot and a half long — was always stored handily inside the teacher's desk drawer. It could by applied only to the open hand. I applied it to Jim's. The news spread through the community, and a cry of relief went up from all the mothers of the other boys. *At last* they had a teacher who would *do something* about Jim. This I heard from Ellen as well as another woman whom I later visited. Trouble on the school ground was replaced by games of softball. My reputation as a good teacher was secure. This was not something I learned at Normal School!

Most of the children walked to school, but one little first grader named Sophie, came on horseback. The horse provided to her by her family was a large workhorse. It had a very wide back over which a huge saddle had been secured. The stirrups dangled down, unused. Sophie sat astride this saddle, her little hands holding tightly to the reigns, her short chubby legs stretched out sideways into the air, and her lunch box hooked over the saddle horn.

On arrival at school she would slide off the horse, then tie it to a fence post. No problem. However, at the end of the school day, getting back up on the horse, for her trip home, was something else again. Taking reigns in hand, Sophie would climb the fence post. But the moment she made a move to swing her leg over the back

Ernest Park School class picture.

Chapter Three / Ernest Park School

Ernest Park School.

of her horse, he would take a step away. Sophie would jump down from the post, scolding and pushing this big animal back in place, for another try.

The boys thought this whole scene was hilarious and shrieked with laughter. Undaunted, Sophie would try again, with the same result. Finally the boys' good natures would take over. A number of them would hold her horse, allowing Sophie to throw herself onto his back, and away she would go, reins in hand, lunch box secured over the saddle horn, and her chubby little legs sticking out sideways.

That spring, mumps spread through the school. My brother and I, as well as sisters and many friends, had all suffered through mumps as a children. I knew the symptoms. Noticing the large, lopsided swelling on the neck of one of the older girls, I sent her home with a note to her mother. Sure enough, she had mumps. Every day I unobtrusively examined the necks of my remaining students, and every day I sent another child home. About a quarter of the children ended up with mumps. In those days, parents were relieved when their young children caught this disease. It was usually mild in children, but had dangerous side effects for teenagers and adults.

Another vivid memory I have of this school is of mud. Spring must have come early that year, bringing with it warm days that thawed the roads in a hurry, turning them into muddy quagmires. Dirt roads in Alberta were a mixture of dirt and clay, without a trace of gravel. Cars were fitted with tire chains to avoid getting stuck in a major way, and walking was next to impossible.

Getting to school under these conditions was a challenge. My only hope was to step on whatever vegetation could be found at the side of the road. But eventually the road had to be crossed. The mud would suck down my boots like quicksand, making it almost impossible for me to move my feet without stepping out of my boots. I remember this happening many times but I must have persevered, because there never was a time I failed to a get to school more or less on time. *That* I would have remembered.

It was hard to say goodbye to the children at Ernest Park School, and to Ray and Ellen, whom I suspected I would never see again. It had been a good two months. I headed back home with my footlocker, my book box, and a good feeling that this teaching job had been reasonably well done. As I boarded the bus for the long trip home, I *looked forward* to my next teaching assignment, whenever and wherever that might be.

Chapter Four

Lone Ridge School

District of Wetaskiwin , 1943

I signed up to teach in my third one-roomed country school in the spring of nineteen hundred and forty-three. Just as they had the year before, the Wetaskiwin School Board hired me to finish the school year for a teacher who needed to leave. *Why* this teacher needed to go with only two months left in the school year was a mystery to me. Again, someone suggested a nervous breakdown. Not very encouraging!

This new school was in the same general area as the one in which I had taught the year before. Once again, I took the two buses from Edmonton and was left off at a designated spot by the side of the road in the middle of nowhere. But, this time no one was there to meet me. Alone with my book box and footlocker beside me, I fought panic and wondered what I should do. Before long, an angel, disguised as a local farmer, drove up, stopped, and asked if I needed help. After finding that I surely did, he gathered up my stuff and had me on my way. Fortunately for me, it was common knowledge in this community that the school was expecting a new teacher, and everyone knew where I was to stay.

We drove off the highway, then down a rough country road before turning into some woods on a trail that was scarcely wider than a footpath. After passing a number of smallish barnyard buildings housing chickens, pigs, and livestock, we reached the back of a small two-story house, which was to be my home for the next two months. This choice of residence had been decided by the aforementioned school board, with help, no doubt, from the community.

My new landlord and landlady turned out to be Lou, age 19, and his sister, Jean, age 16. Their mother had died many years before, leaving their father to care for the two young children. The year before I came to live with them, he too had died, leaving the teenagers to care for themselves and work the farm as best they could, with the casual help of an uncle, who lived not far away. Thinking back on this now, I suspect that the person in charge of finding a place for the teacher might have felt it was a good idea to add a helpful older adult to this household, but if so, it was lost on me. In the first place, I had no knowledge whatsoever of running a farm, and in the second place, it would not have occurred to me to offer advice to Jean, who appeared to be doing just fine on her own.

Actually, I was filled with admiration for the two of them for assuming such a colossal undertaking with cheerfulness, courage, and confidence. Jean seemed much older than sixteen. Circumstances had forced her to grow up in a hurry. We quickly became friends. In retrospect, I am sure that there was nothing I could have done that would have been more helpful to her than what I was actually able to do — be a supportive friend and companion.

My bedroom, an upstairs space under the eaves, was just big

Chapter Four / Lone Ridge School

enough for a bed, a small bedside table on which to put a coal
oil lamp, a chest of drawers, and my book box, which as before,
doubled as a bookcase. There were hooks along the wall for clothes.
When I blew out my coal-oil lamp on my first night, I heard a
scritching and scratching in the general area of the ceiling. It
sounded like mice — *many* mice. After groping for matches I quickly
relit the lamp (as quickly as it is possible to light a coal oil-lamp
in the dark) and examined every inch of the ceiling for cracks or
holes. Nothing.

The room had been decorated with wallpaper that covered every
inch of it, walls and ceiling. In fact, whoever had papered it had
started at the floor, gone up the walls and across the ceiling, and then
down the opposite wall, using continuous overlapping strips until
the whole room was covered. There were no cracks or spaces between
walls and ceiling for *anything* to creep through without tearing the
paper. Reassured, I once again blew out my lamp, ignored the noise,
and went to sleep. It had been a long day.

The next morning, I mentioned this strange phenomenon to Jean
and Lou. They were distressed.

"We meant to warn you about that," they apologized. "Some time
ago we noticed a large opening under the eaves of the roof. When we
climbed up to see if we could fix it, we saw that the attic was filled
with bats. We had also noticed that our barnyard was free of flies and
mosquitoes, so we decided to let the bats stay. "

Every evening at dusk, the bats swooped around the barnyard.
They ignored us and we ignored them, and how wonderful it was
not to be bothered by flies and mosquitoes — a major problem in
rural Alberta.

The only problem I had with Jean was her cooking. I'm sure I could have done something about this had I tried, but I chose not to. Actually, it was not her *cooking* that was at fault but her *menu*, because she had only *one*, for dinner that is. Jean's father had not been much of a cook. All he had known about cooking was what he had remembered from watching his wife. When she died, he had taken over the cooking, teaching Jean all that he knew.

For every dinner, during the two months I was there, we had fried, home-cured ham (very salty), boiled potatoes, a canned vegetable, and canned fruit for dessert. I was rarely there for lunch, but typically, farm breakfasts and lunches consisted of what was left over from the main meal of the day before, plus eggs. One day Jean and I went to Wetaskiwin, the closest town, where I took her to a restaurant for dinner. She ordered pork! I asked her if she ever cooked any meat besides pork, and she replied, "Sometimes when the harvesters come in the fall we have a roast of beef."

I had arrived on a Sunday. On Monday morning I set out early for my school, which was a short distance away. I got there to find that the door to the school building was locked, and there was no one in sight. The only sign of life I saw was a man on a tractor, far away, plowing a field. Looking the school over, I noticed a stick of firewood propped up against a side wall, under a window. This suggested a possible alternate way in. Sure enough, the window could be pried open. I glanced around to be sure I was not being observed, then climbed in.

Before long, a small boy came through the same window. He looked at me with astonishment, and then jumped back out. Soon he

Chapter Four / Lone Ridge School

was back with another boy, then another, and another, all following the same wordless pattern. I was beginning to think the entire school was made up of small look-alike boys.

I was told that Morris, one of the older boys, was supposed to come early with a key to open up the school, but he was often late. When 9 o'clock came — time for school to begin — and Morris still had not appeared, I taught my first lesson: how to pick a lock. Actually, I had never picked a lock before, but I had heard it could be done with a hairpin. Not having a hairpin, I smoothed out two paper clips and poked at the lock from the inside, while the children poked at it from the outside.

Wonder of wonders, the lock sprang open. Everyone cheered! Soon order was restored, and each of my new pupils was in his, and yes, *her* desk. At this point Morris, who turned out to be somewhat mentally disabled, walked in with the key and was persuaded (though reluctantly) to hand it over to me.

Since this was my first day in their school, I asked the children to write me a letter detailing anything they would like me to know about themselves, such as what they liked most or least about school. The first graders could draw me pictures. Here is what a child named Wesley wrote:

Dear Miss Clark,

This isn't very encouraging, but I'm one of the worst fellows in this school. You can ask anybody what I did last Halloween. I am the slowest person when it comes to arithmetic. I can't apply myself. My best subject is social studies. I hope this school won't be as hard on you as we were on our other teacher. We're a reckless bunch. You can ask anybody what we did last Halloween.

Sincerely yours,
Wesley Montgomery

Not very reassuring, but Wesley turned out to be a sweet kid, and I would never have characterized him or his buddies as "a reckless bunch. " I asked my landlady if she knew what he had done the previous Halloween. She revealed that he and some other boys had pushed over an outhouse. I'll bet it wasn't even his idea.

On the way home from school that day, I saw a small, strange-looking, pink animal rooting around in the weeds by the side of the road. I stood looking at it with amazement, having no idea what kind of animal it was. A car came by and stopped. A young man got out. He started to tease me about the novel way I had opened up the school that morning. It turned out he was the farmer I had seen on the tractor. He had witnessed the whole scene, to his great delight, and I would later discover that he loved to tell any interested party about my expertise in breaking into a building and picking a lock.

Next, he turned his attention to the strange little animal. With great amusement at my ignorance, he informed me that it was a newborn pig. I have no idea what ever became of that poor little lost pig, or how it got there in the first place. It must have been taken *somewhere*. It is so strange to me how some inconsequential incidences from the past can be stamped indelibly on my memory, while others are lost forever, as the years pass by.

Chapter Four / Lone Ridge School

Lone Ridge School class picture.

I liked being with the children at Lone Ridge School, and they liked me. I remember reading books to them, singing, and refereeing softball games during the noon hour.

One day, when everyone was quietly doing whatever they were supposed to be doing, the class suddenly sprang into action. All the children were out of their seats, running, and yelling. One boy was tearing around with a broom, and others wielded rulers.

"What's going on?" I shouted.

"A gopher! A gopher!" someone shouted back.

A *gopher*? I thought. All this fuss for a poor little gopher that had somehow gotten into the school? There was nothing to do but open the door and wait it out. After a few minutes, the terrified little creature escaped out the front door. Thank goodness the children had not killed it — especially in front of me. This accomplished, the children settled down in their seats and, without comment, resumed

Students in the classroom, busy with their schoolwork.

their schoolwork. How the gopher got into the room, I was never to know, but I wondered. Was my predecessor *that* afraid of gophers?

Another day, I was sitting quietly behind my desk in front of the class, while everyone was seated and working. This was a rare occurrence because, with eight grades to teach, I was usually working with one group when the rest were busy on their own. Suddenly, a shrill whistle broke the silence. I quickly looked over the class. All twenty-five of them were busy with their assignments. Then it happened again, even louder than before. I looked over the class once again, and someone giggled. That did it!

"Who is making that noise?" I demanded in a stern voice, knowing immediately that this kind of question is a no-winner. Then, having committed myself, I asked it again.

Seated near the back of the room a boy who raised his hand, with a smile on his face. Since he was often a ringleader for mischief of one kind or another, I lit into him, but he kept smiling, which raised my ire to a new level. When I had run out of things to say, he finally spoke, still smiling. In fact, to my discomfort, *all* the children had smiles on their faces.

"Miss Clark," he said. "I think you should know that a *gopher* is making that noise under the floor of our school."

I started to laugh. The more I thought about it, the funnier it got. Soon everybody was laughing with me. I never knew a gopher made that kind of sound! I had never heard a gopher make any kind of sound. I apologized, for accusing them so unjustly, and thanked them for adding to my knowledge of wildlife in Alberta. We all settled down and went back to work.

After I had been at this school for a month, my sister Nancy, who was twelve years younger than I, came for a two-week visit. Mother was needed in Vancouver because of a family crisis, and my other sister, Mary, had declared that she couldn't stand the thought of living with Nancy for that long without Mother there to keep her in line! Mary was only six years older than Nan, which makes a big difference at that age. In any case, I was delighted to have my "baby sister" come. She would sleep with me in my little room and be a fourth grader in my school.

My only worry was that Nan might turn up too well dressed, and look out of place in the classroom. The girls wore drab, ill-fitting clothes that had seen many scrubbings and patchings. Children's clothing had a low priority in farm budgets. I urged mother to pack Nan's oldest and most worn-looking outfits. In spite of this, she was far and away the most attractively dressed girl in the school. Not that

My sister Nancy (far right) with a group of the girls on a rainy day.

it mattered. My students took her in, and enthusiastically showed her the ways of this country school in particular, and rural life in general.

One day at noon, while the children were playing softball, a gopher popped up from his underground home, stood upright on his front legs, and viewed the players. Nancy, enthralled, cried out, "Oh! Look at the grasshopper!"

The other children, stunned, stopped the game. Then one of them said in a kind, understanding way, "Nancy, that is not a grasshopper. That is a *gopher.*"

One mother told me later that her son had come home with this story, ending it with, "That poor little city girl didn't know the difference between a grasshopper and a gopher."

Nancy, hearing this, was disgusted. "I *do* know the difference between a *gopher* and a *grasshopper.* The names just got mixed up in my mind. After all, it was on the *grass* and it was *hopping.*" An understandable mistake!

Another understandable mistake on Nancy's part caused

Chapter Four / Lone Ridge School

considerable concern on Lou's part. There was a huge pig on the farm, housed in its own pen. Nan was fascinated by this pig and kept referring to it as "the old sow." Lou, who was very shy, and a man of few words, sidled up to me one day in obvious embarrassment, saying he felt I should talk to Nancy about the pig. "The old sow," he explained, was actually "the old boar," and it was a mistake he felt needed to be corrected, not just overlooked!

Toward the end of the school year, the Wetaskiwin School Board organized a track meet — a yearly event for all the schools that could get their children into town. The father of one of my pupils offered to take us to this meet in his big grain truck. We all piled in for the fifteen-mile or so ride. Twenty-eight kids loose in the back of the truck generated great excitement! This was probably the only field trip the school ever had. It was a laid-back event, loosely organized, but with ribbons for all participants. A fun day!

After lunch, the wind started to pick up, growing stronger by the minute. Suddenly, it grew to hurricane-like force, picking up the topsoil from a newly plowed field next to the athletic park, and blowing this soil over everything in its path. The sun was blocked out and the day grew dark. It was hard to see past one's feet, and hard to breathe. Scarves, lunch bags, jackets, and debris of all kinds sailed around us.

I was appalled. It struck me with tremendous force that I was responsible for all these children who had disappeared from my sight and were goodness only knows where. I wasn't sure where our truck would be parked, or where our driver was. He had gone off to do his own business in town. But farm children are used to taking care of

45

themselves. Somehow they found each other, as well as their teacher, the driver, and the truck. All accounted for. No one was particularly upset, just sad that his or her field trip had been cut short. No one was shaken in the least — apart from the teacher!

Another school year had come to an end, and I hated to say goodbye. I had grown to love all these children, and had become very fond of Jean and Lou. I wanted so much for things to turn out well for them the following year, but I was never to know. It had been a good two months all. Now it was time to go home.

POSTSCRIPT

When working on this memoir I wrote to my sister Nancy, asking her what she could remember (if anything) about her visit. She wrote me the following letter.

Dear Fran,

You said you were writing up your recollections of life in the one-room school days. You asked if I could remember anything about being at the school with you. You said two weeks. I'm sure it was a month! I've always told people it was a month! Time didn't go so quickly in those days! Anyway, I remember quite a bit about that experience. I remember the house. It only had four rooms. You came into the kitchen, which was a big room where we ate, although I am a bit hazy about the eating part. There was a parlor beside it. We never went into that room. The bedrooms were up the stairs from the kitchen. You went up a few stairs, then turned and went into a hall. Ours was the first room, and there was another one for

Chapter Four / Lone Ridge School

My sister Nancy (center) with Jean and Lou.

Jean. I have no idea where Lou slept! There wasn't much room in our bedroom except for the bed. You must have had someplace to work, but I don't know where. There was a dresser, and Jean put a pitcher of water on it for washing. I cannot remember if there was electricity. The stove wasn't electric, and there was no refrigerator. Nothing was cold. I certainly can't remember Jean using power to make butter, and Lou certainly milked the cows by hand. And there was definitely no bathroom. We had to use the outhouse. But it seems to me that Jean provided us with a potty for use at night. I don't think I ever had to use it. But it was *cold* first thing in the morning going outside.

We had to walk down a drive to get to the road that led to the school. All I can remember about that road is the ruts. It was hard walking, and the boys used to have trouble riding their bikes. I walked with the kids. Perhaps you went on earlier and started home later.

I was never afraid of the kids. They were very nice, and nobody teased me. We all carried our lunches. Sometimes I would be very

Nancy helping Lou around the farm.

brave and cut across the field to the farm. But sometimes the cows would be out in the field, and they really scared me. I can still close my eyes and see those cows all looking at me, and some of them even moving toward me!

The school day was interesting, mainly because my sister was the teacher. I didn't call you "teacher" or "Miss Clark," just nothing! I really can't remember anything in particular that we did in the way of activities or class work. I think I remember spelling, but that stands to reason, for you likely knew what a terrible speller I was and figured I could use a lot of extra work. I can remember you reading to all of us. There was one story from *Alice in Wonderland* in which there were terrible puns. I just groaned or laughed, and no one else did! As usual, recess was the best time, and I really fit in because I was pretty good at softball and could hold my own. There was an outhouse, of course, one for the girls and one for the boys. There was also a barn, and I think a couple of kids rode horses to school. We'd eat our lunches before going out at noon. I can't remember if I liked my lunches or not, but I do remember the terrible taste of the milk. Lou said it was because it was unpasteurized. I wouldn't drink milk at Aunt Frances' farm (many years before), and she was a bit miffed, saying I shouldn't be able to tell the difference. I tried it, and she was quite right. Lou's cows must have been eating something that affected the taste of the milk. I forgot my lunch pail one day, or it wasn't ready, and Lou brought it for me and left it under the wire fence by the school. Another time, my jar of milk was broken, or the lid came off, and my lunch was ruined. I was so upset because Jean's jar was broken.

One weekend, an admirer of yours came by and took you and me with him while he graded the roads. I remember sitting on the fender of the tractor while we bumped along those rough roads. One time I bounced so hard I slid off the fender, and this guy, quick as a wink, pulled me back up. I think his name was Charlie.* I can't remember the important parts like whether there was a blade on the front or he pulled some kind of plow. I just remember the tractor.

I don't think Jean and Lou had horses, because I have no recollection of being put on a horse. Yet, they must have had a workhorse, as I doubt they could afford a tractor. They had pigs, and I got to feed them the slops! I can't remember getting eggs, but there must have been chickens.

With love,
Nancy

* Charlie was the farmer I had seen plowing his field the first day of school. I suspect his only admiration for me was for the way I could get into a locked schoolhouse!

Graduation, University of Alberta, Spring 1944.
I received a Bachelor of Arts degree with a major in
History and Philosophy.

CHAPTER FIVE

ELK POINT SCHOOL

"End-of-steel", 1944

In the spring of nineteen hundred and forty four, I graduated from the University of Alberta, receiving a Bachelor of Arts degree, with a major in History and Philosophy. With teaching experience in three different schools, a university degree, and better still, a recommendation from a friend, I managed to land my third two-month, end-of-the-school-year teaching job. This time, it was to be in a *two-room* school in a town, instead of a *one-room* school in the country. This was a great step up the teaching ladder — at least in Alberta, circa 1944. My benefactor, Doreen, who had been teaching high school in Elk Point for two years, remembered that I might be available when the need for a substitute teacher materialized. Doreen and I had known each other since high school.

Elk Point is about a hundred and thirty miles east of Edmonton and a few miles north of the North Saskatchewan River. It was at the "end-of-steel," which meant there was just one railway spur connecting it with Edmonton. Beyond Elk Lake, to the north, south, east, and west, was bush country, occasionally interrupted by small farms. The train, and *only* the train, brought people, as well as all the mail and supplies, to the town. It arrived from Edmonton each Monday, Wednesday, and Friday, then carried on a little farther to some turn-around system of track, and returned the next day to take people, mail, and supplies from Elk Point back to Edmonton. Six times a week the train rumbled through Elk Point, coming or going. On the seventh day — the Sabbath — it rested.

The arrival of this train was the major event of the day. It was heralded by its whistle, which grew joyfully louder and louder as it approached the town. It seemed as though everyone who could rushed away from whatever they were doing to join the rest of the townspeople at the station to find out what and whom the train had brought that day. It provided a wonderful opportunity to visit and gossip.

On one particular day, the train brought *me* to Elk Point, (population 300, more or less). As I stood in the space between two cars, waiting for the train to slowly stop at the station, I was astonished to see such a large group of people crowded onto the small station platform. They all seemed to be looking at *me!*

I was trying to shake off the temptation to look back and follow the line of stares, when the Superintendent of Schools, accompanied by my friend, Doreen, materialized out of the crowd and helped me off the train. He led us to his car and whisked us (as well as my footlocker and book box) away from the station to my boarding place, which as before, had been arranged for me by the school board. I was to share a room with Doreen. In response to my inquiries about why there was such a large crowd at the station, and what they were trying to see, my hosts explained to me that the arrival of the train was always a big event. Think nothing of it.

Some time later, Doreen clued me in. The crowd at the station that day had indeed been larger than usual. Apparently there had been considerable consternation about finding a suitable person to fill the vacancy at the school. As the superintendent had departed to Edmonton on his mission to hire a new teacher, he had let it be known that the job might be hard to fill, but he would do his best. On his return, he reported — with his fingers crossed behind his back, I should hope (the mischievous wretch) — that he had found someone who was a good enough teacher, as far as he could tell, but he was sorry to say that she was not very attractive, had a gimpy leg, and was blind in one eye. After all, beggars couldn't be choosers. No wonder everyone had been looking at me! This was my first and probably *only* shot at celebrity!

My teaching activities in that first-, second-, and third-grade classroom went well, with no highs memorable enough, or lows serious enough, to make permanent impressions on my mind. But a few events did stand out.

Next to my boarding house, lived the only doctor for a radius of fifty miles or so. He had an office in his home, but he made regular visits to outlying places, among them, the country schools scattered about wherever one was needed. (I believe it was the law that if eight or more children lived within three miles of each other, the community had to provide a school.) Once every three years, this doctor visited all of these schools to vaccinate the children, in grades one through three, for smallpox. Not long after I arrived, the time came for him to immunize my class.

53

One day this doctor appeared, unannounced, at the doorway to my classroom and proceeded to take each of my students out in the hall, one by one. I don't remember dealing with permission slips, or arranging for parents to be present. I don't think that was deemed necessary. In fact, I would be surprised if there was not some kind of law requiring the vaccinations.

Presumably, the town had been notified. In all probability a handwritten sign had been tacked up in the post office, There might have been a news item in the local newspaper. Without copy machines, sending notices home was no small task, and rarely done. Besides, everyone in the town heard by word of mouth whatever they needed (or wanted) to know.

Smallpox was a disease that was greatly feared. Survival rates were low, and those who did survive carried ugly scars on their faces and bodies. In my younger days it was quite common to see people thus disfigured, and we all knew it was caused by smallpox. The live vaccine used in those days was injected into the arm or thigh, by way of a tiny scratch, which became an infected-looking sore before healing to a small, round, white scar, about 1/4-inch in diameter. Far from complaining, or worrying about any possible harm the immunization might cause, every parent rejoiced that medical science had come up with this wonderful gift for his or her child.

By the end of that day, all twenty-five of my brave little six- to eight-year-olds sat in front of me with scratched arms; no fuss, no tears, at least none that I heard or saw. During the week that followed, the scratches turned into red sores that looked worse daily. The doctor came back, once, to check on the newly vaccinated children, and declared that all was fine. Hard to believe! The children rarely complained, but it was all I could do to keep my mind on my work, as I gazed on row after row of wounded children. When I saw those inflamed little arms fade to a normal pink once again I was tremendously relieved.

One morning Doreen and I emerged from our house to see about thirty or more American-Indian men, women, and children camped out on the doctor's lawn. I learned that this happened from time to time. Whenever this particular tribe decided that it was time to have the doctor check the condition of their health, they turned up at his doorstep, and waited for him to appear. If he was too busy, or not at home, they set up camp in a vacant spot outside of town and returned in the morning to resume their wait.

This time, they sat in front of the house for a day or two as the doctor attended to their needs, then disappeared as quietly as they had appeared. The townspeople were used to this, but for me, a city girl, it was truly amazing.

Another memorable event at Elk Point was a wonderful with some young people from the local United Church. We started out very early in the morning carrying a bag breakfast.

After walking a mile or two, we ascended a steep prominence in order to see the sun rise over a distant hill, and to watch the morning light sparkle on the waters of the North Saskatchewan River, not far away. This river had its origin in the Rocky Mountains, ran through Edmonton, then all across the prairies to empty in the Gulf of St. Lawrence.

On another day, a friend of Doreen's, drove a few of us through miles of lovely virgin woods to a crystal clear lake. We drank its clear, pure, water, before going swimming, using the bushes for dressing rooms.

One night, the whole town participated in an honest-to-goodness square dance, held in a big barn-like building where a local caller kept us moving at a break-neck pace. This was a new experience for me, but I was never made to feel foolish while stumbling through the steps. The dancing started at about eleven p.m. and broke up around three in the morning. I remember the time it ended, because I had never in my life been up and out that late. My experiences in late-night-to-early-morning partying had been few and far between up to then, and have been since then, if the truth be known!

The last day of June came all too quickly. The train whistled itself in one day, shunted around up-track a ways, and returned the next day to take me, as well as my footlocker and my book box, back to Edmonton. A departing train holds little excitement for onlookers, but for those on board, thinking about what awaited them at the "end-of-steel" can be all consuming. I was about to enroll in the University of Alberta's summer-school program, which would eventually lead to a Bachelor of Education degree. This commitment was weighing on my mind as I stepped onto the train in Elk Point. The next school I would teach in was out there somewhere, waiting to be found, with, hopefully, no more than one or two grades per class, and this time, for a full year.

CHAPTER SIX

JOHN RUSSELL ELEMENTARY SCHOOL

Camrose, Alberta, 1944

My next — and last — teaching assignment was with the Camrose School Board, teaching first grade. A friend from my university days, Elizabeth Kerr, was a long-time resident of Camrose; her father had been the United Church minister there for many years, and Elizabeth was a teacher in the town high school. It was wonderful to be commissioned in a town where I had a ready-made friend from the first day I arrived as well as the benefit of easy transportation for visits home to Edmonton via train.

This time, the school board took no responsibility for my living arrangements, but through Elizabeth, I learned of a family who wanted to board the new teacher. In fact, they had arranged to board two of us. The other teacher turned out to be a girl I knew from Normal School named Doris. Neither of us realized, until we arrived at the home of our hosts, the Cassidy's, that we would not only be teaching in the same school, but also sharing a room and a bed. People seemed to assume in those days that a double bed meant two-person occupancy!

The Cassidy's cottage.

Our room was very small, with only just enough space for clothes storage. Any preparation for teaching had to be done at school. Doris informed me that for all of her life, at least so far, she had shared a room and a bed with various members of her large family — as had I with mine, for that matter. She forewarned me that she had not managed to get through a year of this type of living arrangement without having a major fight with whomever her roommate happened to be.

Because I rarely got into big fights over anything, I was not too worried. As it turned out, the fight she anticipated never happened. We became comfortable friends, who gave each other the needed emotional and physical

Chapter Six / John Russell Elementary School

space to make the living conditions work out well for both of us.

Camrose had grown considerably over the years. A two-room elementary school had been replaced by a large building, but by the time I appeared on the scene even the big school could no longer house all the children. The original little two-room school was pressed into service again, this time to accommodate only the first grade students — all seventy-six of them. The rooms

My roommate, Doris.

were small — much too small for the thirty-eight children who had to squeeze into each of them. But there was a large basement and a good-sized playground, just for us.

During the first day, I rearranged my classroom, by pairing up desks side by side, to create aisles wide enough to walk between the rows of children. The front desks were touching mine, but this allowed enough space at the back of the room to circle a few chairs for small-group work.

In those days, kindergartens were not part of Alberta school systems. None of the children had been to school before, and few, if any, knew the alphabet or could read numbers. Parents did not consider it their responsibility to introduce their children to reading

Fellow teachers.

or math. Few parents even *read* to their children, unless it was something they personally enjoyed doing.

Phonics was not the current method for teaching reading. Instead, children were taught to read phrases after they were able to recognize a few single words. This was reflected in all the pre-readers and seat-work material, and was the method taught to us in Normal School. Today, it is being vigorously challenged. For whatever reason, my thirty-eight first graders dragged their feet when it came to reading. Few managed to get through the first grade book. Just before the end of the school year, I accepted a position, which would begin the following September, with the Ontario Religious Education Council. This meant that I would not have to face the second grade teacher when my poor readers were handed over to her. I had the feeling I was skipping town just in time!

I realize now how many things I, as well as others, could have done, to help the children. If anyone needed an extra hand in the

Chapter Six / John Russell Elementary School

Relaxing in the Cassidy's back yard.

classroom, *I* did, and most of the mothers of these children were home alone, not working. They would have been more than willing to volunteer. But it was just not done. Even when my own children went to school many years later, I was never asked to help with any classroom activity — only to provide extra supervision on field trips. Parents, even then, were seldom, if ever, invited to participate in school activities, except to watch a performance of some sort, or to provide refreshments. As a former teacher and as a parent, I note with envy and amazement the involvement that my daughters and their husbands have in the education of their children.

I could have given simple homework, such as finding objects that begin with an A, etc. All this basic beginning reading activity, which is now done in preschools and kindergarten, had to be done in the first grade classroom, with no follow-through at home. Parents had no way of knowing what was going on in school, and many of the children, who needed help the most, could get missed in classroom drill, because of the exuberance of others. There was very limited communication between school and home. With no way to copy an assignment, how would homework have been sent home?

I have no memory of parent conferences, if indeed they were even scheduled. The whole system, beginning with our so-called training at Normal School, seems crazy to me now, but hindsight is incredibly revealing. At the time, I truly believed that if the children were not reading at a beginning second-grade level by the end of the year, it was all my fault. And, in many ways it was.

No parent in Camrose ever walked children to and from school. The streets were safe, and only "babies" (according to the children) got walked! The children arrived on their own. If a mother came to give a measure of support on the momentous first day of school, she left her child at the gate, or nodded briefly to me at the door. Mothers had no place in the classroom. Everyone knew that, especially the children.

On this first day of school, three little friends came together as a trio, with no accompanying adult: Susan, age five; Lily, age seven; and Deloris, age six. The age at which one could legally begin school was six-years-old, which meant that Susan was a year too young. It was legal, but not usual to start at seven. Six was the customary age.

I learned from the children — not from the parents, or the principal — that the reason the school board had granted Susan permission to begin school at age five, was because her sister, Lily, was deaf. Susan, and their friend, Deloris, would act as interpreters. Great! Besides thirty-six regular first graders in this very small classroom, I had one child who was underage and another who was

Chapter Six / John Russell Elementary School

deaf. Neither the Normal School nor the University had given me the slightest hint as to how to teach a deaf child, or any child with special needs for that matter.

In fairness to the principal, or school board, or whoever approved this Lily-Susan-Deloris team, I doubt that anyone understood how profoundly deaf Lily was. As far as I knew, she had never been tested by an audiologist. In any case, medical records were not required for school entrance. Lily's family treated her as completely normal, and it was hard for the casual observer to notice her handicap. She was a bright, happy child, who kept her eyes on everything that was going on, recognized routines in record time, and was typically the *second* person in the room to stand, or sit, or take out a pencil, etc., when asked to. June and Deloris had developed their own set of signals, which Lily followed instantly.

She was no trouble whatsoever in the classroom. I loved her

Lily (left) and June.

and longed to help. If only I had had a group of say, fifteen children, instead of thirty-eight, and even a beginning knowledge of sign language! It would have been great for all of us to have learned some signing. As it was, Lily learned a few basic words and how to print them, but I knew, for her sake, that she had to be in a special school the following year.

Many of the children, including Lily and her friends, went to a Sunday School. On meeting their teacher, one day, I asked her if it was hard to have Lily in her class.

"Lily?" she said, "Why, she is no trouble at all. She sits quietly and listens well."

"I just wondered if her deafness was a problem," I added.

"She's *deaf*?" the teacher replied, in amazement!

One weekend I persuaded Lily's parents to let me take her home with me to Edmonton, and have her tested by a hearing specialist. I needed some ammunition when confronting the school board, and Lily's family, about her future education. The specialist confirmed that she was totally and irreversibly without hearing, and provided me with the necessary documentation.

After the appointment, Lily and I went to a coffee shop for lunch. I wondered how I could find out what she would like to eat. No problem! Without hesitation, she scanned the pictures of food that could be ordered, pointed to a hamburger, soft drink, and ice cream, then scanned my face for confirmation or disapproval, all in half the time it would have taken a hearing child to reach the same decision.

It was difficult to convince the school board of Lily's needs. I had made some inquiries as to the district's responsibility for the education of children with special needs, and discovered that if

Chapter Six / John Russell Elementary School

John Russel School class picture.

the district did not have special schools for these children, they were required to pay all expenses for the children to go to a school recommended by the province. This included room, board, and transportation. In Alberta, the school of choice for the deaf students was a residential school in Montreal, about 3,000 miles to the east! Their brochure described the program in glorious color.

When the school board got wind of my scheming, they sent an inspector to meet Lily. I remember in detail the scene that followed. The inspector waited for the children to be dismissed, then sat behind my desk. The trio — Lily, Susan, and Deloris — sat in the front desks, as if frozen in space, looking at him. He politely called Lily up. She did not respond. Then, not so politely, since he was used to instant obedience from young children, "I *said*, come *here*."

This was too much for Susan and Deloris. They instantly used their own brand of sign language, which was to poke Lily on either

Children along the playground fence.

side with a forward motion. She sprang to her feet and placed herself before the inspector, looking intently into his face.

"What is your name?" he said kindly. She did not respond.

"I said," he repeated in a loud voice, "WHAT IS YOUR NAME?"

He still received no response from Lily, though her eyes studied his face intently, as she desperately searched for a clue as to what he wanted from her. Susan and Deloris were getting visibly agitated, but what could they do? Even if they got her attention, by some means, they knew she could not answer him. They sat like stones, suffering silently for their friend.

The inspector's patience ran out. "It's obvious the child hears nothing," he announced, as he looked rather accusingly at me.

Lily was still standing at attention before him. Looked at her, as if he had forgotten she was there, he said in a disgusted sort of way, "Oh, go sit down."

She stood unmoving.

Chapter Six / John Russell Elementary School

"I said," he repeated, "GO SIT DOWN!"

Again, this was too much for Susan and Deloris. They jumped up. Lily saw this action out of the corner of her eye and caught a familiar sign — frantic small beckoning motion of hands. She quickly turned and went back to her seat. The inspector left with no word to the children, and a perfunctory "Good day" to me. I presumed the school board got the message: The child hears nothing.

I gave the impressive brochure to Lily's parents, who were stunned at the mere thought of sending their child off to live far from home. I was disappointed in their reaction. At the time, it seemed to me that it would have been a wonderful opportunity for Lily, but now that I have been a parent and a grandmother, I can appreciate the agony that it would have been.

I think Lily's parents made the right decision. Her father was a

Recess in the yard.

A view of Camrose.

postal carrier. He got a transfer to Calgary, where there were classes for the deaf. They were probably not up to the standard of the school in Montreal, but this truly loving, accepting family remained intact. The only sad note was the break-up of that very special trio.

At the end of October, when the days grew shorter and shorter, and the temperature dipped lower and lower, our large basement room was a godsend. Hooks for coats, knitted headgear, mitts, and scarves, lined three sides of the room. A piece of heavy string with a hook on one end and a clothespin on the other could clip together a pair of overshoes or rubbers, to be tied to the hook.

On relatively mild winter days the children could dress themselves, but when the thermometer sank below zero it was necessary for teachers of first-grade pupils to help the process along. Miss Green, the other first-grade teacher, and I would watch our seventy-six small children struggle to pull extra stockings over

Chapter Six / John Russell Elementary School

shoes, jam them into overshoes; find the extra sweater that went
under a coat; and put on a head covering of some kind. For the final
element — the scarf — they came to us for help.

We declared that there were seventy-six ways to put on a scarf.
Each mother had her own way of doing this, and each child insisted
that his scarf follow the system established for him. It could go from
front to back, or back to front; over the coat or under the coat;
crossed before, or after. It went around the neck, over the head, and
inside the hat, or *over* the hat. It could cover the chin and nose, or just
the chin; and variations of all the above. We helped the children dress
twice a day, because they walked home for lunch. Many of them had
many as six blocks to walk. This would have been dangerous for them,
if they were not well protected from the bitter cold.

During the three coldest months — December, January, and
February, when the days grew even shorter and the nights longer,
Children would leave home at eight thirty a.m., in darkness, and
arrive home at four thirty p.m., in darkness. However, the dark held
few fears for children growing up in this northern climate. It was the
way of life, especially for city dwellers. I remember, as a young child,
walking home alone from an after-school activity, watching with
delight how the streetlights sparkled up the snow. Every window in
every house had been lit up, and above them the stars had begun to
come out. There was a magical quality to the night.

One day, during our mid-morning recess, a small boy from my
class came running in, crying. He said he had been swinging very high
on our swing, gone over the top, and fallen off! This is actually not
possible, but he was visibly shaken. While listening to his tale of woe,

**My C.G.I.T. (Canadian Girls in Training) group.
I am pictured in the back row, center.**

I noticed another little boy standing in the doorway, stunned, in need of help. Running to him, I saw a nasty-looking lump growing on his forehead. The result of being hit by the swings's (wooden!) seat.

I gathered him in my arms, called to Miss Green to keep an eye on my room, and ran with him a city block to where I had seen a doctor's office. I left the child in the doctor's care and heard nothing more that day. The child returned to school the following day with a huge lump on his forehead, but otherwise seemed fine. What a commotion that would have caused had it happened today — and rightly so! Miss Green and I should have been taking turns watching the children during recesses, and the swing seats should have been made of rubber or canvas.

Chapter Six / John Russell Elementary School

Living in Camrose gave me the opportunity to become part of
the community, in a way that none of my other away-from-home
experiences had. I sang in the church choir; led a C.G.I.T. group
(the acronym stands for Canadian Girls in Training, a weekday club
sponsored by Protestant churches); belonged to a book club; and
played bridge once a week with Doris and two other teachers. This
was a terrific forum for catching up on all the gossip concerning
school matters. I developed a wonderful friendship with Elizabeth
Kerr, and was free to go home to Edmonton, thanks to the train,
without needing others to help me with transportation.

A Canadian Pacific Railway line ran between Edmonton and
Camrose. I could walk the two long blocks to the station on a Friday
evening, returning close to midnight on a Sunday night. I will always
the walks back to my boarding house, on cold, crisp, black nights,
with only a few streetlights to guide me, and the sky brilliant with
stars from horizon to horizon.

By the summer of 1945, my career as a public school teacher was
over. I was to begin a totally new work experience with the Ontario
Religious Education Council in Toronto, Ontario. This led me in a
new direction, and was a major fork in the road my life was to take.
What a blessing I chose the path I did! It eventually led to marriage
with my husband Dick, and as a result of this union, I have three
wonderful children, and five beautiful grandchildren. But I am
forever grateful for the enriching experiences I gained during my
years of teaching in Alberta classrooms.

PART TWO
THE STORY CONTINUES...

ONTARIO, CANADA
1946 – 1949

NEW YORK, UNITED STATES
1949 – 1950

CHAPTER SEVEN

THE ONTARIO RELIGIOUS EDUCATION COUNCIL

Ontario, August 1946 – August 1949

Toronto, Ontario was my destination — an exciting one, since I had never been east of Manitoba. With considerable trepidation I boarded a Canadian Pacific transcontinental train, and on the way considered my new "career" as Children's Work Secretary for The Ontario Religious Education Council (O.R.EC.), whatever that might turn out to be. My only assurance of measuring up to this job, was that the "powers that be" seemed convinced I could do it. I wished I had the same confidence in myself. Time would tell!

The Rev. Mr. McLean, who was the general secretary of the above organization, as well as my boss-to-be, met me at the station. After a quick tour of the city, he deposited me at the rooming house, where I was destined to spend the year ahead. This was on Huron Street, about a mile north of the Ryerson Press building on Queen Street, where I soon would be working as one of a team of "professionals" in Christian Education.

I had asked a friend of a friend of mine, who had recently moved to Toronto, to keep her eyes open for a room for me to rent. She noticed a "Room for Rent" sign, not far from where she herself lived, and inquired within. The landlord, a youngish man, asked a lot of questions about this friend of hers who needed a room. When she told him that I was coming to work for a religious organization, he was impressed, and promptly agreed to hold the room for me. Much later I found out that he had just ousted a couple causing him no end of grief, but decided, on the spur of the moment, to take a chance with someone associated with the church!

My room was on the third floor and under the eaves of the roof. It was small, but big enough for a single bed, a chair, and a low chest-of-drawers which doubled as a table. Two teenage girls from London, England, occupied the slightly larger room next to mine. Their father, a doctor, had sent them to Canada, to keep them safe from the bombs that were dropping nightly over London in this time of war. These girls were having the time of their lives, enjoying this newfound freedom from parental supervision. Cynthia was still in school, but Louise had a job — painting flowers on china goods, such as pitchers and vases. We became good friends.

In the hall, at the top of the stairs, was a hot plate for the making of simple meals. It was placed on top of a narrow cupboard, which we used for storing the few pots, dishes, and cutlery we owned. There may have been a small sink there as well. If not, there could have been one in our rooms, though I can't remember this important detail. Surely we didn't have to go downstairs to the second floor for water from the bathroom we shared with five other renters on that floor? Maybe we did. What I do remember was a low dormer window off

Chapter Seven / The Ontario Religious Education Council

our third hall, that led to a somewhat flat roof top. This was a great place from which to view the city, eat a snack, or just cool down on hot evenings.

My first few days at the office were spent going through the copious files left by my predecessor. In this way, and only this way, I began to figure out what this new position of mine was all about. That same day, my boss — E.R. McLean, (or E.R. as everyone in the office called him) — handed me my first assignment. I was to go to a small town, not far from Toronto, stay the weekend with the minister's family, and preach the sermon for his congregation on Sunday. All I remember about this assignment was worrying myself sick over the sermon, which I practiced in my head during the train ride to my destination. It must have met expectation, (which, in any case, was probably not very high!) As time went by I discovered that ministers in these small towns cherished the chance to have a Sunday off from preaching, and were not about to be critical toward whoever gave them that break, (Nor were their congregations!)

A sequel to this story came two years later. I received a letter from a minister in a small town north of Toronto, asking me to come to his church on a certain weekend, stay with him and his family, preach the Sunday sermon, and meet with his Sunday School teachers. By this time such an assignment was all in a day's work for me.

He met me at the bus stop, and told me how much his family was looking forward to seeing me again. They had enjoyed my previous visit so very much. I had no idea what he was talking about.

77

I had never been to this town before, didn't recognize him, his name, or knew anything about his family. When I got to his house, his wife and children greeted me as a friend, but were strangers to me. I pretended to know them. It was only when I saw some toys, of all things — one of them triggered a memory in my mind, and suddenly it all came back to me. This was the family I had stayed with on that first assignment of mine. The whole experience had been so traumatic that I had blocked it out, completely!

The most wonderful part of that first year was making new friends. Margaret Robb, our Girls' Work Secretary, took me under her wing. She introduced me to Marjorie Peck, who was a don at the university. Everyone I met, one way or another, was involved in some aspect of church youth-work, and I felt I had found my place in life, which included a wonderful group of "kindred spirit" friends.

Later on, that year, I had the privilege of being sent as a delegate to a conference on Religious Education of Children, being held in Detroit. A postcard that I sent to a friend, who later showed it to me, stated, "This week-end I'm off for Columbus Ohio for an international convention. It is all very exciting. Margaret Robb is bringing another suitcase full of clothes. I can hardly wait!"

Often the whole staff, or sometimes just a few of us of us, would have our evening meal at a restaurant not far from the office. Usually Wilber Howard, our Boys' Work Secretary, would be with us. He was black. We were a close-knit staff and completely color blind as far as Wilber was concerned, but every once in a while I would notice someone looking rather askance

Chapter Seven / The Ontario Religious Education Council

at us. After all, this was the nineteen-forties when the races were pretty well separated.

During September of that first year, E.R. arranged for us four "Secretaries" of the O.R.E.C. to go on a "field trip" through a section of Northern Ontario. We were to meet with, and hopefully help, some of the far-flung churches associated with us, but with whom we seldom had personal contact. Our group consisted of E.R., Wilbur Howard, Margaret Robb and me. We drove north through Muskoka, past Sudbury, then stopped at Timmins, Cochrane, Kapuskasing, and even crossed into Quebec, to a small town whose name I have long forgotten. Here we were told by one of our hostesses, that we were sleeping over a gold mine. Margaret Robb was intrigued by that statement.

"Sleeping over a gold mine" " she exclaimed. "What a wonderful title for a sermon!"

I wonder if she ever used it?! Margaret was often asked, as all of us were, to be a guest preacher when "on the road". I remember her saying that it didn't seem to matter to a congregation whether you were tilted toward the liberal, rather than the conservative side of theology as long as you inserted a number of "alleluias" and "praise the Lords" as you preached your sermon!

The most memorable part of that Northern Ontario assignment was driving through the most beautiful scenery I had ever seen. We passed huge maples and oaks, dressed in glorious fall colors, and reflected in numerous lakes. Coming from Alberta where the fall season provided us with acres of brilliant yellow leaves (from the prevailing poplar trees), with a splattering of red here and there — truly a sight to behold in their own way — but nothing like this.

At each church we visited, we followed the same general pattern. There would be a general meeting to which were invited all interested town folk from whatever churches were within driving distance. Those who came were mostly Sunday-School teachers or any who might be persuaded to be one. E.R. would open off the meeting with a short greeting, explaining our purpose in being there, which was mainly to acquaint them with the purpose of out organization which was to be of service to Sunday Schools in any way we could. Margaret Robb would follow with a rousing hymn sing, before Wilbur Howard's book report.

I remember one particular book report he gave. On the table before him, he had placed all the leadership-training guides we had. But after introducing them, from behind him he brought out a number of disreputable looking Bibles, which he had collected from various rooms in the church building. With tongue in cheek he started to talk about them.

"Now here is the handy loose leaf variety," he would announce, "it allows you to isolate any page you want. And this edition," he continued as he held up a book without it's covers, "let's you get right to the text without having to open the cover." And on he went in a similar vein, making the point, of course, that our children need to see that we treat the Bible with respect.

Miss Semmens, of the United Church of Canada, recalled asking for a bible at a church where she had been a guest speaker. There was a great scurry around the church to find her a bible. When one was produced, it had printed on its cover page, "Presented to this hotel by the Gidions"!

Chapter Seven / The Ontario Religious Education Council

I was shy one course toward a Bachelor of Education degree from the University of Alberta, so one of my projects that first year in Toronto was to complete my studies. I needed to have taken the course *The History of Philosophy and Scientific Thought* — and arranged to meet this requirement by correspondence. The only help I received from the university was a list of suggested books to read. About half way between my office and my residence, was a public library. Whenever I was free from other commitments, I would walk from my office to this library, (after stopping at a restaurant for dinner), and read books on philosophy, taking copious notes. More than once I laid my head down on my arms, and rested my eyes. This always brought the librarian to my side. "Sleeping is not allowed in the library," she would inform me. Apparently resting weary eyes was not allowed either.

Toward Spring I made arrangements to sit for the exam in an empty classroom at the University of Toronto. One of the dons, a friend of mine, sat with me to make sure I didn't cheat — such as looking something up in a book, (heaven forbid!) On opening up the exam papers I discovered, to my dismay, that the course was named *The History of Philosophy and Scientific Thought*. Somehow I had missed, or forgotten, the *Scientific Thought* part. Fortunately it was an essay type exam, and I could choose to write on three out of six or so topics. I avoided all the topics that had the word "science" in it, and managed to pass the course. How well I have no idea — and didn't care! My goal was to PASS, and to qualify for my Bachelor of Education degree. Which I did.

Margaret Robb resigned in the spring of that year. This started a search for a new Girls' Work Secretary, and I thought about my friend from Camrose, Elizabeth Kerr. During her growing up years, her father had been the minister of the United Church in Camrose, Alberta. She was currently teaching in the high school, but over the years had helped, one way and another, with all aspects of church life — especially as it concerned young people. I was overjoyed that the council called her, and that she accepted.

We made plans to share living accommodations. This set me looking for a new room to rent. By the time Elizabeth arrived, I had located a possible living place for us. It was a room in an old house on a pleasant tree-lined street, not too far from public transportation on Yonge Street. We decided to move in.

Our landlady and her husband lived on the ground floor of this house. They rented the second-floor rooms, all of which were fairly large. There were four rooms, including a kitchen. Elizabeth and I requested the largest room. I cannot remember how we managed to furnish it. What I do remember is acquiring a used couch from somewhere. I can still see the delivery-men trying to get this heavy piece of furniture up to our room, via a curving staircase. And how frightened I was that they would drop it, and in doing so, ruin the stairs, as well as the antique looking banisters. This couch became my bed. Elizabeth slept on a cot placed against the side-wall. We ate our meals at a card table in the middle of the room, but most of our preparation for leading groups, or giving speeches for one reason or another, we did on the floor, with papers and books spread around us.

On the way home from the office we would stop at a grocery store, to buy something for our dinner, and before eating we took turns saying grace. Elizabeth always said the same one, "For what we are about to receive, may we be truly grateful." I argued that this grace sounded as if we found it hard to be grateful. In the end we would examine the meal before us. If it looked especially good, I would say the grace. But if it was just "so-so", then Elizabeth's fit the bill!

As the year went by Elizabeth and I had fewer and fewer evening meals together. She was in great demand by C.G.I.T groups throughout Toronto, as well as in towns far and throughout Ontario. She met with leaders of teenage girls, spoke at rallies, and Mother-and Daughter banquets, and helped in the organization summer camps. But when she came back to our "home" for the night, we would share our day's events — (especially the amusing ones) — sometimes far into the night.

Two other rented rooms were on our floor. A newly married couple, Hugh and Bernice Hamilton, occupied one of them, and a middle-aged widow, Louise, the other. We became reasonably good friends, though had little time for just being together, except for the few occasions we all happened, at the same time, to be trying to get a dinner together in our community kitchen.

Hugh and Bernice Hamilton, as well as Louise, occupied side-by-side rooms at the end of the second floor. One morning Bernice asked us if we knew of the expression, "You could hear a pin drop". "Well," she said, "last night Hugh and I were quietly sitting and talking together, when to our dismay, we heard a pin, or something that small, drop in Louise's room next door. We examined the wall between us, and discovered it was but a single sheet of plasterboard! That's how our landlord had created an extra room. Louise couldn't have helped hearing everything we ever said to each other!"

Elizabeth and I had very few (if any) friends turn up at our living quarters, but one day a male acquaintance whom Elizabeth had known from her University of Alberta days, came to Toronto, and contacted her. She invited him to visit us, and in due course he found our house, and made his way up to our second floor living quarters. He had been a close friend of Elizabeth's beloved fiancé, Lt. Gordon Pybus, who had lost his life during World War II. They had much to talk about, and many shared memories.

I decided to make myself scarce by going across the hall to our kitchen, and doing some much-needed ironing. Suddenly our landlady appeared. It was eleven p.m. When she saw all the lights on, me ironing in the kitchen, and Elizabeth talking to a boy in our bedroom (also our dining room, living room and study) she became livid.

"Ironing at this time of night!" she yelled at me, "Entertaining a man at this hour!" she yelled at Elizabeth, "He has to leave. Now! I don't allow this kind of goings-on in my home!"

Elizabeth's friend bid me a hasty good-bye before she accompanied him to the front door where they made arrangements, I suspect, for a less stressful meeting place. I put away the ironing board.

Many years later, when I was married and living outside of New York City, I had the occasion to recall this episode, when my landlady had yelled "Ironing at this time of night?" Only this time it was my husband. The lights had suddenly gone out, and he had stumbled up the stairs from our basement, where he had a professional photographic lab.

"What are you doing?" he yelled at me, "Ironing at this time of night? You have just blown out all our fusses!" As it turned out the

Chapter Seven / The Ontario Religious Education Council

lights were blown out all up the east coast and into Canada. And it had not been my fault!

Separate Schools, Protestant, Catholic or Jewish, each with its own school board, were common in those days. Toronto, as in many Canadian cities, had "Separate Schools", and funded by taxes. This allowed a limited amount of religious education to be given in schools. The protestant clergy decided that their effort, in this direction, would be to provide teachers with a list of bible passages to be read — one a day — to their individual classes. This meant, of course, that someone had to come up with an appropriate list of verses. The solution was to call a meeting, once a month, to which all Protestant clergy were invited, urging them to bring along a list of appropriate verses for different age groups. Since they found selecting scripture for the very young, rather daunting, they invited me as a "Children's Work Secretary" to help out.

These monthly meetings were held in a boardroom located in the largest Church of England in Toronto. It was an oblong room filled with an enormous long and narrow boardroom table, around which were large, comfortable, armchairs. One day, arriving about ten minutes late, I opened the door to look down on this table, around which were seated about ten to twenty clergyman, many of them in clergy garb. All looked at me, and all attempted to rise to their feet, in deference to a lady's presence! Their "close to each other" armchairs made this difficult. I quickly slipped into a chair left empty for me. The men sat down to the loud sound of scraping chairs. Finally, when all noise ceased, the chairman cleared his throat. The meeting resumed. I resolved never to be late again!

85

As summer approached that year, I developed a sinus infection, which settled in my chest. I barely made it to the train that was taking many of us to our Leadership Camp, being held at beautiful Lake Simcoe in Ontario. Fortunately the camp nurse took me under her wing, and I was able to fulfil my leadership duties, but only just.

With no break in between I was on my to way to attend another Leadership Camp, being held on the shores of Lake Memphremagog, in the province of Quebec. On the way to the train, (which was to take me to this new destination), the camp nurse insisted that I see a doctor about my cough. We stopped at the first doctor's office we noticed as we passed along the way. After hearing my story, he gave me some pills to suppress the cough. I boarded the train late that evening, and fell into a deep sleep, thanks to the pills, which seemed to suppress my cough by putting me to sleep!

I woke up to the commotion caused by the train preparing to stop in Montreal. Here I was to be met by someone who would transport me to the campsite. I threw myself together, as best I could, staggered off the train, and was met with great enthusiasm by a couple who had been given this "honor", which would involve not only transporting me to the camp, but tapping my brain about leadership matters along the way. Instead, I promptly fell asleep in the back seat of the car, and didn't wake up until we arrived at the camp.

Here I experienced the best thing to happen to me in weeks. I was placed in a cottage with an older woman, (I believe her official duty was "camp mother") who immediately saw I was in trouble, and took me under her wing. Between meals, and after the time it took to conduct my two daily leadership sessions — one on child psychology, and the other on curriculum — my wonderful roommate saw to it

Chapter Seven / The Ontario Religious Education Council

that I slept for hours each day. My only other memory of that camp is of swimming (mostly floating!) in the beautiful waters of Lake Memphremagog, upon whose shores this camp was situated, and marveling that only these waters separated us from the United States of America.

On arriving back home from this camp Elizabeth informed me that her parents had decided to move to Toronto, from Vancouver, where Dr. Kerr had retired. They had bought a house on Eglington Avenue. Elizabeth and I were urged to move in with them. By the end of the summer we were in our new home.

That fall I continued to struggle with poor health. Early in November my boss, E.R. sent me home to Edmonton to recuperate. I was not to return until after Christmas. All I remember about that visit home was spending a wonderful Christmas week, with my family, in Banff National Park. I returned to Toronto in good health, and renewed my residency with Elizabeth's family.

Shortly after my return to the Eglington Avenue house, Elizabeth and her mother staged a fashion show for me. Mrs. Kerr had made a "basic black" dress for Elizabeth, which Elizabeth modeled for me. She disappeared into a bedroom and returned to model the same dress which was now given an entirely new look with a scarf or collar or whatever. This went on for some time. I was stunned not only by Elizabeth's new wardrobe, but by the easy, loving, yet interdependent relationship between her and her mother.

The leadership-training assignment I remember most vividly that year involved a trip to Lindsay, Ontario. All my life I had heard about

Lindsay. My mother had spent several years of her childhood there, at the home of her mother's sister.

When I boarded the train to Lindsay, it seemed I had stepped into the past. This train swayed from side to side as we traveled along. The ceiling lights were a row of swinging coal oil lamps. I had assumed I could buy a sandwich on the train, since my experience had been that someone would come along selling lunch items, if there was no dining car. Our car was far from full, but at lunch-time (by our watches) out came the lunch bags. On seeing that I had not planned for this, several people offered to share their lunches with me. This made for a friendly, spontaneous, social gathering.

I had started to feel a headache coming on, while traveling on the train. By the time I reached the house where I was to be billeted, my head was in the throes of a full- blown migraine. Since my reason for coming to Lindsay was to meet with Sunday-School teachers in that area, and deliver a course on "Childhood Psychology", there was nothing I could do but carry on. It was winter, with snow on the ground, and I remember being sick to my stomach into a snow bank on my way to the school where the teacher's meeting was being held.

Waiting for me were about twenty teachers who had come from many churches, in and surrounding Lindsay, to hear what wisdom, regarding the Christian Education of young children, this "professional" from Toronto could offer them. I had been asked to talk about the characteristics and abilities of different age groups, as well as what children in each group could be expected to understand. Knowing this I decided to begin by describing in very broad terms the different abilities and needs of preschoolers (age five and under), primary (age six through eight) and junior (age nine through eleven).

Chapter Seven / The Ontario Religious Education Council

This took about an hour before I called for a recess.

The first person to come up to speak to me during this break, introduced herself as the local doctor. She proceeded to tell me that she knew I was in trouble physically, and wanted to know what the trouble was! I shared with her that I was trying to cope with a severe migraine. I don't remember what she said, or did, for me, but when our fifteen-minute recess was over, my headache had disappeared. Like magic! The next hour or so I continued to lecture, then led a discussion about appropriate Religious Education for each age group.

When the class was over my wonderful doctor came up to me again, this time to ask me about one of her patients — a young girl who was in trouble. She was refusing to go to school, or to leave her house. There was nothing physically wrong with her. This doctor wondered if I would meet with her and her mother to help sort out the problem. I was appalled. In no way was I qualified to help in this way. Had I really come across as a professional psychologist? I had been following a simple study guide, which I augmented somewhat, from past experience with young children. We talked about the child's problem, but my only advice to her, was that if the situation did not right itself, given time, and following suggestions from the teacher, the mother and child should seek help from a professional clinic in Toronto. I wish I knew the sequel to this part of my story.

The Matthew family (my Grandmother's family) had lived in Lindsay. My mother, as a young child, had spent extended visits there, to be with her grandparents and aunts. As I was growing up, she had told me many stories of these visits. Amazingly, Mother's "Aunt Bessie" still lived in Lindsay in the same house where she had spent so many of her childhood years. I went to see her. She was an old woman, beautifully dressed and "put together", but it was her hands that fascinated me the most. While she talked to me she stretched them flat out on the table before her. I remember "Granny" (my maternal Grandmother, Frances Lucy Wolverton) doing the same thing in exactly the same way.

A few years before I joined the staff, there was a time when O.R.E.C. had invited Marian Anderson (a famous black singer) to come to Toronto, in order to support us financially by performing a fund-raising concert. She accepted. But a problem arose. No hotel in Toronto would accept her! My Grandmother's brother, Albert Edward Matthews, was currently the Lieutenant Governor of Ontario. When he and his wife Maude heard of this problem they invited Miss Anderson to be a guest in their home. Later, during visit to their home in Toronto, Aunt Maude told me what a privilege it had been to have her, and told me about the interesting conversations she had had with Marian about her life.

My mother's aunt, Isabel Stewart, lived in Hamilton, a city close to Toronto. When she heard I was living and working in Toronto, she invited me to spend a day or two with her and her husband Harold. She eventually suggested that I come any time I needed a break. I appreciated this so very much, and one weekend accepted her invitation.

Apparently, Aunt Isabel had no idea what I was doing in

Chapter Seven / The Ontario Religious Education Council

Toronto — only that I had some kind of job associated with the church. But some of the women in her "Mission Circle" knew about me, or at least about the O.R.E.C. Finding out I was in town, they

"Aunt Bessie" (Sarah Elizabeth Ryley, standing) and her sister, "Granny" (my maternal grandmother, Frances Lucy Wolverton, seated). Photo taken on Granny's 80th birthday, in the parlour in Lindsay, 1940.

asked me to be the main speaker at one of their meetings. The subject was to be "The Missionary Education of Children".

Aunt Isabel was upset. I think she worried that I was could not meet the standard of excellence expected from her group, and might let down the family — or something like that. But I liked this subject and enjoyed talking about it. My presentation went over well, to her great relief, I suspect, (she had attended the meeting). The following is an excerpt from the church news section of the local newspaper:

The Missionary Education of Children was the timely subject of two addresses by Miss Frances Clark, Children's Work Secretary of The Ontario Religious Education Council. For several years the decline of the Mission Band department has been of deep concern to the superintendents, and all those interested in the young people of our churches. The large place given to Miss Clark on the program was the attempt to give leaders a fresh prospective...

Most of my time with the O.R.E.C. was spent meeting with Sunday school-teachers, in small towns throughout Ontario, helping them deal creatively with their curriculum. One time a fairly large group of teachers of junior-age children were holding a meeting in Toronto, and I was asked to talk to them about "non-projected" visual aids. In other words pictures, time lines, posters, and so on. Especially items that the children themselves could help create. At least that was the help I felt was (or should be) needed.

To that end, in somewhat of a hurry, and with whatever material I could lay my hands on, I created a poster or two, an illustrated

Chapter Seven / The Ontario Religious Education Council

time line, a "movie projector" (made out of a cardboard box through which rolled a series of pictures to illustrate a story) and so on. After my presentation one of the teachers in the audience came up to me and said, "Thank-you so much for your talk. It just goes to show what a person can do with no talent whatsoever." — !

Elizabeth spent a good portion of her time helping to organize and find leadership for teen-age girls' camps. At that time there were no church camps for "juniors" (ages nine through eleven). Miss Semmens, the Childrens' Work Secretary for the United Church of Canada, did not believe in camps for children of this age. In her opinion they were too young for a "sleep away" camp. "Over my dead body will there be camps for Juniors — and there will be!" she would declare.

Since my so-called expertise was confined to this age group and younger, I was never involved in camps. However I had been a volunteer camp counselor may times in the past, and I missed this experience. As summer approached I asked Elizabeth if she could find me a girl's camp to direct. She did.

Early in July of that year I was on a bus, leaving Ottawa, and heading toward the shores of the St. Lawrence River, where I was to take over my duty as a camp director. This camp was being held on a small island in this very large and famous river. Unfortunately the bus broke down half way to my destination. We waited until another bus was sent out from Ottawa to rescue us, but it took an hour or so to reach us. Luckily I had a book to read — *My Sister Eileen*. This I remember because it was really amusing, and I would burst out laughing, from time to time, in this otherwise quiet bus. No one else in the bus was laughing. Far from it!

Eventually we were rescued, but I arrived several hours late, to the great consternation, but relief, of the local camp committee. Their other consternation was that the boys' camp, which was finishing up their last day, had been almost rained out. Should the girls' camp be cancelled? The boats that would take the girls to their camp would bring the boys back. Since the weather seemed to be improving by the hour, it was decided to go ahead, and pray that the sun would shine once again.

I met the girls, about thirty of them, while waiting on the dock for the boys to return. This seemed a good time to collect registration forms, and I discovered to my surprise, and dismay, that all of them were twelve years or younger. This was a "Junior Camp". What would Miss Semmens say should she ever find out! My problem was that all the helpful material, provided to me by Elizabeth, especially bible-study, was meant for twelve years and up. On the other hand, who better to lead a children's camp than the Children' Work Secretary!

This campsite was actually a provincial picnic site. There was a covered dining area, as well as an adjoining kitchen with a stove, sink, and running water. In this small space the cook, in the rain, had prepared three meals a day for thirty people. She had threatened to leave if there was one more rainy day, but we lucked out. It was great weather the whole weak.

However we ran into problems created by the rainy week. The campers had brought "ticks", as they were called. They were simply cot-sized bags to be filled with straw in order to become a mattress. Unfortunately the pile of straw, to be used for this, was completely

Chapter Seven / The Ontario Religious Education Council

wet, due to the rain the week before. My first lesson to these children, regarding camping, was telling them, that in order to keep warm during the chilly nights, it was important to have as much bedding below one as above. This meant the campers had to double up. One girl's bedding served as a mattress, and her "partner's" as covers. It was lucky these kids were "underage" and therefore on the small size. They took this arrangement in stride, and I can't remember if the pile of straw ever dried out enough to be of any use.

The next problem we faced was dealing with a child who was truly "homesick". She cried non-stop, was really sick, and I sent her home with the person who was scheduled to come daily with fresh milk (and anything else the cook needed). We were down one. But the cook was happy with the coming of sunshine, and the camp mother and I quickly became friends. It turned out that she was the sister of our minister's wife back in Edmonton. It's a small world!

Our campsite left much to be desired. Because it was a provincial picnic area, the four "out-houses" it boasted, were located in four entirely separate areas, in order to service the entire island. Only one was close enough to our camp to be useful. This meant line-ups and waits for a turn. And, since our island was one of "The Thousands Islands" of the St. Lawrence River, we had water on all sides, as this mighty river rushed by. There was an alcove quite near us, where our daily boat landed, that was reasonably safe. Here we could swim, but the children were repeatedly warned to stay away from the river in any other place.

Because the Bible Study books provided to us were not suitable for this age group, I presented the material, in a simplified way, to the whole group. There were three other counselors, each of whom would lead a small group in a discussion about what I had said. In spite of our rocky start, everyone seemed in good spirits during the remainder of our week together. It was hard for me to say goodbye as each group in turn boarded the boat that came to take us in shifts, across the St. Lawrence River, with me in the last sailing.

My last leadership event, as a member of the Ontario Religious Education Council, was at a leadership conference on the shores of beautiful Lake Simcoe. My outstanding memory of this occasion was finding myself leading the traditional "sing-song" after meals. The guest leader at this conference was Dr. Foster Wood from New York City. His expertise was Family Life, but he loved group singing, and was loud in his praise for my ability as a song leader. It so happened that this was an activity I loved to do, but had never had a chance to show off my "skill" in this direction, there always being someone better know for this "talent" at every camp or conference I had attended.

It gave me great satisfaction to be asked to say goodbye in this way. It was to be my last contribution to the work, and life, of the Ontario Religious Education Council of Canada.

During the spring of that year, 1949, it was becoming obvious that this type of Church-work was becoming my life work. To educate myself further, in this field, I applied to attend The Union Theological Seminary, a protestant college associated with Columbia University in New York City. I was accepted as a student in their Christian Education Department. A whole new wonder-filled chapter of my life was about to begin, God willing.

CHAPTER EIGHT

UNION THEOLOGICAL SEMINARY

New York City, September, 1949 – May 1950

September, nineteen hundred and forty nine, found me in New York City to attend classes at Union Theological Seminary's Department of Christian Education. Having worked three years as Children's Work Secretary for the Ontario Religious Education Council, and since it seemed likely that I should continue to work in this field, the time had come to be educated for it. Toward this end I found my way to uptown Manhattan and to McGiffert Hall — a residence that had promised to house me, as well as many other single women and married couples, all of whom were enrolling in classes to prepare themselves for some type of Christian service.

My assigned roommate, Helen Karsh, had already established herself in the spot near the window by the time I arrived at my assigned room. We introduced each other, and quickly became friends. She was from Nebraska, had just graduated with a B.A. from the University there, and was aspiring to be a youth leader in a university setting. I was from Canada with a B.A. and a B. Ed., as well as four year's working in the field of Christian Education. In spite of our difference in age and experience, we became good friends, though we seldom saw each other outside of our room.

At the far end of our hall was a room equipped with a simple kitchen, where students could gather, to prepare a snack or just meet to get to know one another. Union had (and still has) a School of Sacred Music, which attracts students interested in becoming music directors in a church. These individuals usually have beautiful singing voices. Perhaps because of this, one such gathering holds a special place in my heart. A group of about fifteen of us were sitting in this social room talking to each other, when somebody started to sing *O Holy Night*, a song not familiar to me at the time. Immediately everyone joined in, and soon there was an amazing spontaneous rendition of this beautiful carol, complete with alto and descants. A wonder-filled memory for me!

Soon after my arrival, several of us decided to venture a trip "down town". Our goal was to conquer the subway system, and find our way to Union Station, where we could look around and sample the automat. The most knowledgeable among us followed the numerous signs and arrows, which took us to Union Station by way of a cross-town shuttle. It seemed an amazing fete to me at the time, but one I was to master with great ease before my stay in the city was over.

Later on that year, using the subway, I managed to find my way to a church situated in the heart of Brooklyn, where I led a series of five evening lectures, followed by discussion, on the fundamentals of

Chapter Eight / The Union Theological Seminary

teaching the Bible to children. I remember walking several blocks to this church, week after week, always at night, along streets with poor street lighting, and never being afraid.

The course in Christian Education was a disappointment to me. Because I had spent three years working in the field, I gained no new insights or inspiration from this class. In fact it soon became clear (at least to me!) that I knew more about this subject than my teacher. I even managed to have a left over assignment, from my former job, accepted as a grade assignment. It was an outline of a church service, (including scripture, prayer and children's story), which I had prepared for the Ontario Religious Education Council and was to be used by all the churches in Ontario who supported the organization.

However, many of the other courses I took were inspiring and mind stretching. Dr. Harrison Elliott, the senior professor in the field of Christian Education, gave one such course, (the name of which I can no longer remember). It was directed toward those training for the ministry. Our classroom was filled with men, as well as a few women, who were headed in that direction — all seemingly more orthodox, theologically, than Dr. Elliott, to put it mildly. They challenged his every conviction. This made me very uncomfortable, but it seemed not to bother him in the least. Probably "par for the course".

One day I handed in an essay-type assignment, the subject of which I have long forgotten. On returning it to me, I noticed he had written beside a comment I had made: "This shows exceptional insight". This amused me, since this particular comment was a direct quote of something he had said in class! On reflection I suppose the fact that I understood what he was trying to say, and had made a note of it, showed a certain amount of insight!

However, the most valuable insight I did gain from this class, was the realization that if I were to ever find myself in a job where I would be dealing with ministers, I would need to be strong theologically. Actually, I had been in that kind of job before coming to Union, and this had never been a problem — but at least I was now forewarned.

The second course I took from Dr. Elliott was on leading discussion groups. I had led any number of discussion groups in Ontario, or, to be more exact, had spoken on a given subject, and then encouraged questions or comments. Usually there were questions and comments, which I answered to the best of my ability, with the help of others in the group who had their own ideas. To me this was "a discussion". Not so for Dr. Elliott! His definition of a "discussion" was what followed when the leader introduced a subject, after which members of the group, as well as the leader, contributed their knowledge, or asked and answered questions concerning the subject. In the end everyone would know (conceivably) more about the subject than they did before, including the discussion leader, who ultimately had limited, if any, control over whatever conclusions the group arrived at.

The following year found me working as the Director of Christian Education at a church in Dobbs Ferry. The young peoples' group decided to put on a party. Following Dr. Elliott's discussion-group method, I led a discussion group on what the program for the party should be. The emerging plan the group decided on was a program (which included ballroom dancing) that our minister

Chapter Eight / The Union Theological Seminary

vetoed! The reason he gave was that the congregation was not ready for such a party in the church building! After that I decided that the only time I would follow Dr. Elliott's discussion group method was when any conceivable outcome would be one I (as well as the minister and the congregation) could live by!

The class I enjoyed the most was one led by Dr. Muillenberg, on the Old Testament. Most of his emphasis was on the first four books, and especially the book of Genesis. I believe that of all the courses I took at Union, this one inspired me the most. In the years that followed I have drawn upon what I learned there, time and time again.

Two courses at the Teachers' College were required by those working toward a degree in Christian (or Religious) Education. This school was located about a block from Union. The first class I attended here had a name something like *Principles of Education*. The only thing I remember about this class was that it required a great deal of reading from a prescribed reading list. The final exam consisted of a long list of "true or false", as well as "multiple- choice" questions, concerning books that we were supposed to have read, (many of which I had).

After the final exam a document was posted in the main hall of the Teacher's College, listing all the students in the class, with their standing in this test. To my utter surprise and disbelief my name headed the list. At first I thought the names must be listed alphabetically, but there were many others names, farther down the list, starting closer to A then my C (Clark). It looked as if I had

101

actually come first in the class. This had never happened to me before in all the 15 years I had attended schools of one kind or another — nor has it happened since! Wonders will never cease!

The only other class I took at the Teachers' College was entitled *Home and Family Life*, or words to that effect. The professor in charge lectured on various aspects of family life, most of which I was aware of from my own family life, as well as being involved, one way or another, with many other families along the way. The most valuable part of this class was the assignment. We were to begin a "diary" in which we could record events or feelings associated with our own family life, and/or critiques of books we had read from a reading list. There was no final exam. Our grade would be determined by the quality of this diary, which we handed in from time to time, and was read by one of the assistant teachers. They would write comments in the margin, such as "good observation", "why do you feel this way? "Are you sure of this?" "I suggest you might find the following book helpful." And so on.

I was impressed beyond measure by the helpfulness and depth of understanding, shown in the comments, (written in the margins of my "diary") by someone named "Singer". Apparently she had requested my diary every time I handed it in, so that we could have a running dialogue. This was not routinely done. I found this exercise and her comments extremely helpful, and enlightening, as I explored my own family background, as well as my life with a co-worker, Elizabeth, whom I had lived and worked with, for two years. Some time later I read in a newspaper that a therapist with the name, "Singer" had been appointed to a position at Berkeley.

Chapter Eight / The Union Theological Seminary

I suspect it was the same person.

The following year, while working in Dobbs Ferry, I was asked to be one of the "readers" for this class. It was a paying job. Every week I took the train to the Teachers College, in order to collect about 12 or more "diaries", and return the ones from the week before. From the best of my ability, and my ever growing understanding of the human condition, I added comments and suggestions on the margins of these dairies, hoping they might prove as helpful and supportive as "Singer's" were to me.

There were many highlights for me that year at Union. The School of Sacred Music produced a Christmas Carol Program. It was the most beautiful I had ever attended before, or have since. Daily worship services, led by staff or students, were an inspiration, and student meetings revealed the struggles many went through to attend this seminary. I remember one such meeting when a student was carrying on about students who felt they needed some financial help from the seminary. He declared that he himself had never asked help from anyone. Then he paused, thinking for a minute before saying, "of course, my wife is working". There was a great peal of laughter.

"The Second Great War" had just ended that year, but the ravages of war were being felt all over Europe. England, as well as all of Europe, was experiencing food shortages. In an attempt to help out, many students participated in a "meager meal". The regular price of a dinner was fifty cents. Once a week, those who wished to participate in this program, (and many did), could buy a bowl of soup, and a roll with butter, for twenty-five cents, then donate the balance to

103

a student organization that raised and sent "money for food" to Great Britain.

Riverside Church, where Dr. Fosdick was the senior minister, backed up on Union Theological Seminary. One day when I was in residence Dr. Fosdick came to Union to address the students. The only part of his talk that I remember is a story he told of his grandson. Beside the church is a large and beautiful monument to Ulysses Grant, where, it was said, he was buried. This child had pointed to the church and said, "That is Gramps church", then to the monument "And that is Gramps grave"!

To gain on-the-job experience, as well to earn some much-needed money, I was assigned to a first grade Sunday-School class in a large "down-town" Methodist church. This class, of 15 students, was being taught by two youngish, (although older than I), New York City school-teachers. In other words, mature, experienced, teachers. After a few months, I was required to hand in (to Union) a report of what, if anything, I had learned from this experience. This I did.

My supervising teachers got wind of this, and asked to see my report. I should have declined, but at the time, saw no reason not to. Big mistake! In my report I had made some comments concerning the fact that because Thanksgiving is so close to Christmas it is hard to do justice to both. (In Canada, Thanksgiving — a harvest festival — is celebrated the first weekend in October). In the U.S.A. this close "timing", between two important holidays, results, of necessity, that both, or at least one, get short shift. Without meaning to, I may have

Chapter Eight / The Union Theological Seminary

made some other equally incriminating statements. In any case these teachers were incensed!

My last assignment was to write a thesis on any topic concerning Christian Education. I chose "The Use of the Bible with Children". This had always both interested and concerned me. How to teach the Bible to children had come up for discussion, time and time again when I had met with teachers in Ontario. The following "chapter headings" summarize the contents of my thesis.

The need for study into the use of the Bible with primary children
The contribution of Theology
The contribution of Educational Philosophy
The contribution of Psychology
Guiding Principles in the Use of the Bible with Children

I handed the finished document in to Dr. Elliott who, after reading it, passed it around to whomever might be interested. He then arranged for me to attend a meeting, with a few "Union Professors", in order for them to meet, and question me on the subject I had chosen. I was incredibly nervous, but during the meeting it soon became obvious that I knew more about this subject than anyone else in the room! (None of them ever having had much to do with children!) They asked many questions, all of which were easy to answer, before wishing me success in whatever educational experience life might hand out to me next.

Joanne Wesley, a girl from "the south" became one of the friends I made that year. We had shared some classes, and joined with others to explore parts of the city. Over the years we had kept in touch with each other, though infrequently. In the year 1999 we found ourselves both married, with grown children, living within driving distance of each other in California — fifty years after we had graduated from Union! We decided to attend one of the yearly anniversary celebrations of Union graduates. I suspect we were the oldest graduates there! The current staff included many more women, both staff and assistants, than when we were students, those fifty years ago.

One such young woman, a staff member, led a worship service that I will always remember — not the content, but the setting she created. The pulpit, where she was to speak, stood empty. On approaching it, she carried a cloth, a bible, and a cross, all of which she carefully, and reverently, placed on this altar, before beginning to speak. For years I had been leading children's worship services in Sunday-schools, and had always pre-arranged the table. But after this I followed her pattern, allowing individual children to reverently place, and arrange, on our worship table, whatever items we wanted to include.

Toward the end of the school year, I began to come to grips with what I would do the following September — I needed a job. My replacement at the Ontario Religious Education Council was there to stay. No church in Canada had the where-with-all to hire a Director of Christian Education. If a Canadian church could finance two "professionals" the second would be an associate pastor. It looked as if I should have to stay in the United States if I wanted to earn a living in this field. I let it be known that I was available. Before long I had two offers. One was to go to a church in Providence, Rhode Island,

Chapter Eight / The Union Theological Seminary

and the other in to a church in Dobbs Ferry, New York, a 30 minute-drive from Columbia University. I liked the minister, who had come to interview me, and, after a quick visit to Dobbs Ferry, signed on the dotted line, so to speak.

Many years have passed since my year at Union Theological Seminary. But the friends I made while there, and the knowledge I gained, so many years ago, will be with me, helping to sustain me, for the rest of my life.

About the Author

Frances A. Clark Ruttan was born in Ottawa, Canada on July 20, 1920. At an early age her family moved to Edmonton, where she grew up. Upon graduating high school she enrolled in a teacher training program at the Alberta Normal School in Edmonton, during which she taught for several years in country schools as a part of the program. She went on to earn a Bachelor of Education degree at the University of Alberta.

In 1945 Frances was employed by the Ontario Religious Education Council as a Children's Work Secretary and traveled throughout Ontario to help with children's religious educational programs. After three years she decided to continue her education, graduating with an MA in Education from The Union Theological Seminary in New York. Frances then accepted a position as the Director of Children's Work at the First Presbyterian Church in Dobbs Ferry, New York.

Frances married Charles Richard Ruttan in 1951 and raised a son and twin daughters in Hastings-on-Hudson, New York. In 1983 she and Richard moved to Los Angeles to retire. Richard died in 1984, and Frances moved back to Alberta, Canada, where she lived for several years. After receiving news that she would be a grandmother, Frances moved back to the United States, where she now lives with her daughter Molly and Molly's family. This is her first book.

Manufactured by Amazon.ca
Bolton, ON